COOKING
WITH FLOWERS

For my children, Emily and William,
and for Sue

A Fawcett Columbine Book
Published by Ballantine Books
Copyright © 1987 by Jenny Leggatt

Library of Congress Cataloging-in-Publication Data

Leggatt, Jenny, 1937–
Cooking with flowers.

Bibliography: p.
Includes index.
1. Cookery (Flowers) I. Title
TX814.5.F5L44 1987   641.6   86–91804
ISBN 0-449-90252-8

Cover design by James R. Harris
Manufactured in Great Britain
First American Edition: June 1987
10 9 8 7 6 5 4 3 2 1

COOKING WITH FLOWERS

JENNY LEGGATT

FAWCETT COLUMBINE · NEW YORK

CONTENTS

Acknowledgements

Thanks are due to: many friends who cheerfully munched their way through a variety of flower meals and who shared a lot with me, especially Alan and Shirley Wright and David and Penny Jaques; Sarah Wallace, my editor, for her tact, unfailing good humour and friendship; Fauré, Chopin and Mozart for keeping me sane; Mrs Elizabeth Forbes who kindly supplied us with many of the flowers for the photographs from her garden in Oxfordshire; The General Trading Company for lending glass, china and linen for the photographs; David Mellor for lending china for the photographs; Colefax and Fowler for lending chintz; The London Architectural Salvage and Supply Company Ltd for lending marble; Miss Anna Wayte for lending her cups and saucers; T & D Flower Trading, 33 Oaklands, London N21, for letting us use their flower stall for my photograph on the jacket. I would like to thank Christine and Trevor Forecast of Congham Hall Country House Hotel, King's Lynn, Norfolk for letting me use two recipes from their excellent chef, John McGeever. I would also especially like to thank Sue Norrington for her constant support during the final stages of writing this book.

Important Note to Readers

Some delectable-looking flowers are poisonous! Eating them could lead to serious illness or even death. Therefore, it is essential that you consult the Edible Flower Glossary on pp. 138–139, that you eat flowers only in accordance with the instructions contained in the book, and that you carefully follow the recipes and don't eat more than the amounts specified. If you have any doubt about the identity of a flower, don't eat it. Please also note that in the photographs we have occasionally used floral decoration which is not necessarily edible.

Cowslips (*Primula veris*) in England, are not the same as American cowslips (*Caltha palustris*), also called marsh marigolds, which are poisonous. A substitute is given in each recipe.

Marigolds referred to in this book are pot marigolds (*Calendula*), never African marigolds (*Tagetes*).

References to daisies are always to English daisies (*Bellis perennis*) which are much smaller than American daisies.

Tansy can cause contact dermatitis in sensitive people.

INTRODUCTION

It is strange that in Great Britain, with our long tradition of cultivating gardens, we still do not make full use of all the beautiful flowers we grow. We decorate our homes and fill our churches with flowers but we hardly ever think of actually eating them. The wild hedgerows burst with flowers each year but usually we think of gathering only blackberries and sloes and ignore the fat, rosy hips and the profusion of wild flowers that are there for the picking. In the fields and meadows grow many more – wild clary, chickweed, broom, tansy, wild garlic, dill, comfrey, wild basil, wild fennel, sweet cicely, and lots of others.

Flowers have been used for culinary purposes from the very earliest times. The Romans, who introduced so many of the herbs we eat today, also used flowers in their cuisine. Mallows, violets and roses are mentioned by Apicius in *The Roman Cook Book* along with lots of herbs. He even used gladioli bulbs! Pliny describes a dish where the bulbs were 'baked in the ashes and eaten with salt and oil, or pounded with figs'. The Romans used lavender in their sauces and also to flavour honey, of which they were extremely fond. Roses and lavender were 'strewing' flowers in those days and were spread all over the floors of the houses – imagine the heavenly scent! Roman hosts also crowned their guests with garlands of rose buds and used them in cooking, too. Wine was often scented with rose petals; there is a lovely story about the Battle of Cirrha when it is said that the Spartans refused the wine they were offered because it was not scented with rose petals!

Perhaps the seventeenth century was the time in this country when flowers really came into their own. It was then that they began to play an increasingly important part in everyday life. Flowers were imbued with all kinds of significant meanings and Culpeper, writing his herbal at this time, related all plants to astrology and thereby introduced a kind of magical element into the whole plant world.

Shakespeare's plays are full of references to flowers. In *Hamlet*, Ophelia tells us that 'rosemary (is) for remembrance', and Laertes likens love to the violet because they are both impermanent and fragile. This is because the violet blooms so briefly in the spring and never sees the summer sunshine. For this reason it is often associated with early death.

Every household in Shakespeare's time would be hung with great bunches of herbs and flowers drying for winter use. The big houses had great gardens where many kinds of herbs and flowers were cultivated for medicinal and culinary purposes. Some of the most popular were marigolds, gillyflowers (carnations), English cowslips, primroses, violets, nasturtiums, roses, honeysuckle, hawthorn and other blossoms.

The lady of the house would spend a great deal of her time in the garden and in the still room where she would extract, or distil, the oils, juices, flavours and essences of the flowers and herbs. She might make a perfume by steeping highly scented rose petals in fine oil; her elderflower and marigold cream would be the envy of the neighbours who wanted some in order to keep their skin white and free from blemishes. She would have her own store of medicinal receipts (as recipes were then called) and these she would use so that she could administer to her own family and household. Her culinary skills were considerable, for no woman was worth much in those days unless she could cook well! Preserved flowers would appear in tansy cakes, primrose and English cowslip puddings, violet creams, ratafias and strong liqueurs. Gerard, one of the great herbalists, wrote a famous *Herball* which was enlarged and brought up to date by Thomas Johnson in 1633. This became her culinary bible in much the same way as later housewives referred to the indispensable Mrs Beeton's *Household Management*. It is said that Gerard and Shakespeare often used to walk together in Gerard's garden in Holborn. It is quite intriguing to imagine them exchanging ideas about plants and flowers in a country garden.

Flowers were used in countless ways in those days. They were crystallized for decoration and as sweetmeats; pounded into sugar for flavouring; made into syrups and conserves; preserved for jellies and jams and used in sauces. Seventeenth-century cooks made excellent liqueurs from flowers and many different wines. Flowers appeared in tarts and custards; as decoration for meat and fish dishes; fresh in salads and scattered through soups and stews. Many were dried for winter use so that the scents of summer could be conjured up in food and in pot-pourris on cold winter evenings in the draughty houses of that period.

Even in modern China and Japan, flowers are grown in great quantities both for cooking and for making delicately scented teas – lotus, rose petal, hibiscus, jasmine, lily and orange blossom. Both the Chinese and Japanese use chrysanthemums in several of their dishes and these are sold in the markets, washed and ready for cooking. Chrysanthemum hot pot is a favourite dish combining both fish and poultry with vegetables and the petals of dark yellow chrysanthemums. The Chinese believe that chrysanthemum is a *cool* fragrance and therefore good for you and that by eating these flowers you will live longer. Dried lily buds are another popular ingredient for various dishes and these are often cooked with local fungi. The Chinese have a delightful proverb which says 'If you have two loaves, sell one and buy a lily.' The Japanese use the petals of a variety of chrysanthemums and they also boil the roots to eat with soy sauce and sugar.

In the Middle East, roses have always played a special part in cooking. Many dishes are sprinkled with rose water and sweetmeats are baked with it. If you read any book of Middle Eastern cookery you can almost smell the spices they cook with and the distinct aroma of rose water and orange flowers seems to permeate the pages! Think how beautiful a dish of spicy chicken sprinkled with rose water would taste! And how even more perfect it would be decorated with rose petals and served on a large, flat platter so that the scent is spread over a wide area! Incidentally it is said that the first distilled rose water came from Persia where it has been known and used since 140 BC. In the world of edible flowers, it seems, nothing is new!

On the Continent flowers are still used more widely than in this country. French patients, for instance, are often given *tilleul*, a lime blossom *tisane*, in preference to a sleeping pill to soothe them and help send them off to sleep. There are many more herbalists in France and Germany than here. We have only just begun to recognize the fact that flower teas – *tisanes* – can be far healthier and more pleasant than ordinary caffeine-ridden tea and coffee which we still consume in vast quantities, often purely from habit and an inborn insularity which prevents us from experimenting with something new.

Cooking with flowers is infinitely rewarding; apart from their really delicious taste, they are simply the most beautiful things with which to decorate food. A cold dish of stuffed eggs laid on a bed of young sorrel and tarragon can look quite stunning with the addition of a few bright blue anchusa flowers scattered over the eggs. Crystallized rose petals or violets can enhance a sorbet or home-made ice cream while an ordinary green salad can be brought to life by throwing in some brightly coloured nasturtium flowers. Food should be appealing not only to the taste buds but especially to the eye. After all, it is the eye that stimulates and alerts the taste buds. Flowers provide such wonderful contrasts both in colour and texture. They range from the tiny, delicate brilliance of heartsease to the pale, blushing softness of rose petals, from the delicate, star-like, sweet-smelling woodruff to the dazzling boldness of nasturtiums. And then there are those that are simply wildly exotic, like lilies and magnolia.

In England, we often go directly to our own backyard gardens to pick the flowers we need for recipes. In America, it is best to go directly to your local produce market or florist for the flowers indicated in my recipes. Unless you are an experienced botanist or herbalist, selecting the proper species of plant in the wild or even in your own backyard garden can be difficult and sometimes dangerous. Innocuous plants do have their deadly counterparts. For example, cow parsley, a perfectly wonderful and edible plant, bears a striking resemblance to poisonous hemlock. A tiger lily, as edible as it is lovely, should never be confused with other lilies which can cause contact dermatitis. I would advise that if you're not certain which flowers are edible and which are not, use only the flowers I have mentioned in my recipes and only in the amounts indicated. If flowers are designated for decorative purposes only, please follow such suggestion. That which is decorative is not always safe to eat. If you are ever in any doubt, try consulting your local florist or contact the marvellous mail order companies listed in the back of this book. Either source should certainly be able to help you make your dishes as safe as they are beautiful.

In this book I have tried to use flowers in a variety of dishes. Salads are an obvious choice for experimenting with flowers, but few people realize how delicious both meat and fish can taste when marinated and cooked with flowers. Ice creams, sorbets and puddings of all kinds lend themselves to flowers; the delicate petals and buds, with their different shapes and colours, make superb decorations. Both cheese and egg dishes can be enhanced by being flavoured and decorated with flowers, and flower teas, or *tisanes*, are often beneficial medicinally as well as being very pleasant to drink.

Summer wine cups are another way of creating beautiful pictures with flowers. Floating pink and white rose petals in a large glass bowl filled with white wine punch and ice cubes could not be anything other than extremely tempting. Flowers are amazingly versatile and if you use them with imagination they will offer endless delight.

GATHERING, DRYING AND STORING

Since many flowers are not available in dried form it is a good idea to dry your own, starting in the spring and continuing right through the summer. Begin with the early spring flowers like violets, primroses and English cowslips, then proceed to all the glorious summer flowers.

You will find that flowers in their dried form are sometimes not as strongly flavoured as they were when fresh. However, very highly scented flowers like rose petals, violets, lavender and pinks, as well as most herb flowers (especially if you dry these with their leaves) will keep their flavour well.

Always pick flowers for drying at mid-morning on a warm, dry day when the dew has evaporated. The flowers should be open from their buds but not full-blown. At this stage in their growth they have not released too much of their essential oils and will therefore release their full scent when dried. Make sure that the flowers you use are free from insects and that they have not been sprayed with insecticide. It is obviously safest and best to use only those flowers that you have grown in your own garden, patio or window box.

When you have gathered all the flowers you want, remove any green parts and cut off the white heels from all petals. Spread out the flowers on sheets of muslin stretched between two boxes, making sure that the petals do not touch each other. Dry the flowers in a cool, airy place away from direct sunlight. They should be quite dry in a few days and will be crisp to touch. Store them in airtight tins, jars or boxes, not in plastic cartons where they could go mouldy.

If you have dried them properly, the flowers should last throughout the winter. It is such fun on a freezing day to dip into a jar and find the glowing colours of rose petals or nasturtiums, conjuring up the scents of summer in such an enticing way. Think how nice it is to be able to stuff your Christmas turkey with dried nasturtiums, or to make a Christmas cake and fill it with dried violets and rose petals. Hot *tisanes*, sipped in mid-winter by the fire, will not only refresh you but the wonderful flavour of summer flowers will be a happy reminder of warmer days. Tiny dried herb flowers will enhance any winter salad, while just the thought of a hot punch suffused with lavender will make your mouth water! Don't forget to dry plenty of marigolds too, for these traditional pot-herb flowers are essential for all those flower-flavoured winter soups and stews.

CRYSTALLIZING

Crystallizing flowers is one of the most pleasant things to do on a summer's day. It is an easy and satisfying activity and the end result is so pretty. Crystallized flowers make really beautiful decorations for ice creams, sorbets, cakes, fruit fools, fruit salads and meringues. My own family can't stop nibbling them, because they are such crunchy delights just to eat on their own.

Most flowers are suitable for crystallizing; among the most popular are primroses, English cowslips, violets, rose petals, pot marigolds, honeysuckle, borage flowers, lavender, carnations and pinks and all kinds of herb flowers.

There are several different ways of crystallizing flowers and I have suggested some simple methods below. Pick the flowers when they are quite dry and free from insects, but make sure that they have not been sprayed with insecticide. It is best to use flowers that are just open and not full-blown, since these have the best flavour. Remove all green parts and the white heels of petals before crystallizing.

1. Lightly beat egg whites and coat each petal back and front with the egg white. Dip the coated flower in caster sugar, place on a plate or wire rack and leave in a warm place to dry until crisp. Store in an airtight container. Petals crystallized in this way will only keep for up to 2 days.

2. Dissolve a teaspoon of gum arabic (available at most good chemists) in 1fl oz/25ml (⅛ cup) water or a colourless spirit such as vodka. Paint each petal or flower with the mixture, coat with caster sugar and dry on a rack in a warm place until crisp. These should keep for several months.

3. Dissolve 4oz/100g (1 cup) sugar in 2fl oz/50ml (¼ cup) water with a pinch of cream of tartar. Bring to the boil, stirring all the time, until the syrup reaches about 215°F/102°C (take a little syrup between your thumb and index finger and stretch them apart; small threads should form). Dip each petal or flower into the syrup and dry on a rack. Petals crystallized in this way should last a week or so.

4. Beat 1 egg white with just enough icing (confectioner's) sugar to form a thin cream. Brush this onto the flowers, sprinkle on a little caster sugar and dry on a rack. These last only for a day or two.

EAT YOUR OWN WINDOW BOX!

Think how amusing it would be to open your window one sunny day and take a nibble at the flowers growing in your window box! A mouthful of nasturtiums for breakfast, perhaps? The neighbours would probably think you were mad! But how convenient!

Not all of us have gardens in which to grow lovely edible flowers, but everyone has a windowsill and therefore can plant a window box.

First, buy a window box to fit your windowsill. These can be made out of wood, pottery, plastic or polystyrene. If you are worried about whether your windowsill can bear much weight, use a box made from polystyrene. Make sure the window box has holes in the base for good drainage. You might want to buy a tray to put under it; this catches all the drips and prevents your windowsill from getting soiled. Put a layer of broken pottery or stones in the bottom of the box to give the flowers good drainage, then fill the window box with a good potting compost.

Now buy your plants. If you want to grow the flowers from seed, it is best to start the seeds off in a seed tray indoors and plant them in the window box once they are well established. Plant the seeds in a special seed compost and when they have sprouted and are in leaf, thin them out. In a very short time they will grow big enough to be replanted in the window box.

1. Small lavender bush, *Lavandula spica* Dwarf Hidcote, with a height and spread of only 12in (30cm), nasturtiums, chives, basil, marjoram and heartsease.
2. A miniature rose bush (there are many different varieties to choose from; one popular English rose is *Rosa* 'Perla de Monserrat', which grows to a height of 16in (40cm) and has warm pink double flowers), violets, pansies, primroses, sweet woodruff and pinks.
3. Daisies (*Bellis perennis*), English cowslips, red bergamot, anchusa, cornflowers (Bachelor's buttons), chamomile and mint.

There are endless other combinations you could grow, so choose your own favourite flowers; you will be amazed to see how well they will flourish in your window box.

Try to plant both spring and summer flowers so that something is flowering right the way through from April until September. Your friends will be amazed and amused when you open your window and help yourself to some flowers to add to the salad or dessert! Who knows? Perhaps it will inspire them to grow an edible window box of their own!

ENTERTAINING WITH FLOWERS

Flowers are not only used for their individual and unique flavours but as pure visual delights. Entertaining with flowers is an art – a creative activity that has the bonus of exotic and enticing scents.

Some flowers that are edible do not offer great flavours but make up for it by their stunningly beautiful appearance. Food can be decorated with such flowers to great effect, often making guests gasp in admiration. Dishes prepared for friends should look as enticing and seductive as possible so let your imagination fly! Conjure up amazing visual pictures in your mind and then set about making them real by arranging food and flowers together in brilliant combinations.

Some flowers, like roses, carnations and pinks, mallows, hollyhocks, chamomile and sweet woodruff are gentle in colour and fragrance and should therefore be used delicately in food. There are others – such as nasturtiums and lavender – that are bold to look at and strong-smelling and these you can use more exotically.

When you are entertaining try to complement the food you are serving with attractive and unusual floral touches in table decoration. Float flowers in pretty glasses and put one by each guest's place; make a small bunch of crystallized flowers into a napkin posy; arrange place name cards with fresh flowers. You can weave petals through a salad or creamy dessert or scatter them in soups; serve drinks with flower ice cubes (see p. 17). Add flowers to all kinds of wine cups and cocktails, too, and decorate your cakes with both fresh and crystallized flowers.

You can extend your use of edible flowers by decorating the room with them, looping great garlands around the walls or having more formal displays in large vases on pedestals. If you are having a buffet party you might like to garland the table with fresh, edible flowers. This will look very pretty and if you use highly perfumed flowers like lavender, honeysuckle, roses, jasmine and pinks, the scent will be wonderful.

Parties and special occasions demand something different so I have chosen four menus for such times, with ideas for how to decorate the room, the table and the cake. Cooking and entertaining with flowers is a whole new concept and if you are enthusiastic about the idea of using edible flowers in unusual and imaginative ways, you will get a lot of fun and pleasure out of it.

CHRISTMAS

Chestnut and Mushroom Soup with pot marigolds

Spicy Stuffed Flower Turkey with minty courgettes (zucchini), marjoram
carrots julienne, roast potatoes and cranberry jelly

Christmas Pudding with lavender

Mince Pies with crystallized petals

Christmas Cake decorated with fresh and crystallized flowers

Dark, rich chocolates decorated with crystallized petals

Flower Punch – either Wassail or
Chilled Rosé Punch with rose petals

The Christmas Table

Cover the table with your very best damask or lace cloth and then assess
it for size and shape, deciding whether you want to pin garlands around
the side or just decorate the top with flowers. If young children are
going to sit down to the meal, then it is better not to have anything
pinned to the sides of the table. If you want to loop garlands of fresh or
dried flowers around the edges or sides of the table, these can be made
up a day before Christmas. Hang thick cord in loops around the table
and secure with pins covered by bows of ribbon. Use dried flowers for
the main garland, threading through some fresh ones on the actual day.
It is best to make the foundation out of some kind of evergreen like ivy
or holly to give the garland a secure base. The flowers can be wired onto
the cord or just pushed in between the evergreens. Add Christmas roses
or chrysanthemums at the last moment for colour and scent.

The top of the table is easier. Here you can let your imagination take
over! *Place Name Cards* are always fun. Cut out pieces of white or
coloured card and, in beautiful script, write the name of each guest. It is
a good idea to hand over this job to someone who is good at calligraphy,
then you will have a really professional-looking card! To make the card
extra special add a few crystallized flowers to it. Give each guest
different flowers and stick them onto the card with a little egg white or
glue. The card will be something they will want to keep as a memento
of a very special Christmas.

Napkins can also be made to look festive by encircling them with a
garland of tiny flowers – perhaps some rosebuds or freesias. If you don't

want the bother of using fresh flowers, then make a little band with dried flowers. A pretty way to use crystallized flowers is to stick them on to thin ribbon, which can then be tied around the napkin.

When using bigger flowers or sprays, bear in mind what dishes you will need on the table for the meal. You don't want to get the whole table decorated and then find that all the flowers have to be removed to make way for the food! Lay the table with your best china, glass and silver then see what room is left for decorations. Make the table as festive as you can. Use Christmas candles as a centrepiece for decoration. Twist small flowers around the candles or use narrow ribbon decorated with flowers to go round the candle like a maypole. Make sure, though, that your decoration is safe and that nothing can catch fire!

Lay delicate sprays of fresh flowers on the table just before the meal, spraying them lightly with water to keep them fresh. Use holly and ivy as much as you can so that the overall effect is festive and gay.

You might decide to give each guest a tiny vase with a single flower in it – or a small finger bowl in which you float a flower or two. Little touches like this are very important and can make the occasion really special for friends and relatives.

The Christmas Cake

If this is to be the centrepiece then decorate it lavishly with crystallized and fresh flowers. If you want to set a candle in the middle of the cake you can pin ribbons from the top of the candle so that they hang down in loops. Stick little crystallized flowers onto the ribbons, or pin on dried buds and petals. Flowers in any form will give the cake a special appeal – and if you use fresh ones, the scent will be dramatic. See the photograph on page 70.

The Christmas Room

Here you can go to town! If it is a fairly large room, why not hang garlands of holly, ivy and flowers in loops all around the walls. This will look so pretty and you can use dried flowers quite easily for this. Either use a wire base or fairly heavy cord for the garlands and wire the flowers, holly and ivy onto it. Red and green ribbons can hang vertically in rows from the picture rail or the top of the wall where it meets the ceiling. Pin on to the ribbons small sprays of dried, crystallized or fresh flowers. Holly, ivy and fern can be used to great effect – weave all the lovely colours together creating a gorgeous display. This can all be done a few nights before the festive day. You can always add a few fresh flowers to the garlands on Christmas Day and spray with a fine mist of water to keep them fresh.

Don't forget to add flowers to the *Christmas Tree*! Again, like the candle on top of the cake, you can tie long, flowing ribbons from the top of the tree and secure to the ribbons fresh, dried or crystallized flowers. Let the ribbons hang down softly and then decorate the tree as usual with lights, tinsel and silver balls.

You can also, of course, have lovely, large bowls of scented fresh flowers around the room. Decorating at this time of year is a matter of using what is available in the best possible, most imaginative way. The main aim is to create a wonderfully festive room bursting with bright holly berries and evergreens and gorgeously scented with flowers. I have given you just a few ideas but there are thousands more wonderful ways to use flowers and it is up to you to discover this exciting new dimension to decorating!

EASTER

Spring Greens Soup

Stuffed spring fillets of plaice with English cowslips or chive flowers

Mange-tout with primroses
Buttered new potatoes with chickweed
Chicory salad with heartsease

Crème Pâtissière with crystallized violets or primroses

Easter Cake

Basket of coloured flower eggs

The Easter Table

Easter tends to be a less elaborate affair than Christmas or a wedding so the table can be simply decorated with delicate spring flowers: daffodils, primroses and English cowslips. Keep the colour scheme to white and yellow with touches of green. The menu will complement this colour scheme too, so all you have to do is to provide white or green china, silver and glass. Keep the table looking fresh and bright.

A basketful of colourful eggs decorated with flower patterns (see below) would give a splash of colour and you could give each guest an egg to take away with them. You can now buy tiny baskets in the shops. Line these with straw and present each guest with an egg in a basket!

You could make little decorations for each guest consisting of a saucer filled with moss and decorated with English cowslips and primroses. Or you could make a central table decoration out of moss and cover it with spring flowers and possibly tiny Bantam's eggs. Whatever you decide to do let your imagination run freely at this time of year because you have the best possible flowers available to you. If you don't want to stick to the yellow, white and green colour scheme then use violets which are wonderful to decorate with. Give each guest a little bunch of Parma violets secured to their place name card, or, if it's a grander feast, to their own individual menu. The scent will be gorgeous!

Flower Eggs

You can make all sorts of lovely designs by pressing flowers on to white-shelled eggs, then bandaging and boiling them. These softly coloured and decorated eggs are ideal for your Easter table or to give away to friends as presents.

Collect some white-shelled eggs and a variety of spring flowers – primroses, brightly coloured primulas, English cowslips, violets and daffodils. Press each flower on to the egg with its face towards the shell. Bind the flower to the egg with onion skins, which will produce a nice, yellowy-orange effect; or birch bark for soft purples and greys, or spinach leaves for pale greens. Secure these with strips of linen or bandage and bind tightly around the egg. You can tie the strips together or wind thin cord or elastic bands around to make sure they will not come undone.

Put the eggs in a wide pan full of cold water and bring to the boil slowly. Simmer for 10–15 minutes and then run the eggs under cold water for several minutes. Remove the flowers and covering gently, and dry the eggs carefully with a paper towel or soft cloth.

You can lay them in a basket filled with straw or put individual ones in tiny baskets lined with tissue paper. Whichever way you present them they will make an unusual and attractive display at your Easter celebrations. Add some fresh flowers to the baskets too. This will give a pretty spring touch and make the eggs look even more special.

The Easter Room

Again, because Easter is not so grand an occasion as others in the year, you can make the room simple and yet beautiful by just using the flowers of the season decked out in all their glory. What could be nicer than a huge vase filled with spring daffodils? Smaller vases and pretty glasses can be brimming with English cowslips, violets and primroses. The scents will be lovely and help to make the celebratory day a joy.

The Easter Cake

Simnel cake has become a traditional Easter cake nowadays so if you want to make it why not decorate the almond paste top with fresh flowers and serve it on a lovely plate which is also decorated with lots of fresh spring flowers.

You can make Easter biscuits (cookies) too — use a straightforward biscuit recipe and decorate them with crystallized violets and primroses.

WEDDING

Artichoke hearts with prawns and anchusa

Whole baked salmon trout with borage flowers and green mayonnaise
Minty buttered new potatoes
Nasturtium salad

Herb and Flower Cheeses with wheat biscuits

Flower Sorbets and Ice Creams

Wedding Cake

The Wedding

You might decide to have your wedding in a tent in the garden and this will give you a wonderful opportunity for extravagant flower decorations. A tent, with its soft roof and sides, can be made into a garden within a garden, bursting with flowers giving out a glorious smell. Choose the most highly scented flowers you can, depending on the season: hyacinths, violets, jasmine, daffodils and peonies for a spring wedding; roses, honeysuckle, lavender, and lilies in the summer. Decide on where you want your major displays to be and make these bold and eye-catching. In a tent it is often a good idea to have large falling sprays of flowers in each corner, possibly tied with ribbons that cascade down towards the floor. If it is a large tent you might also want some flower decorations on bowls supported by pedestals. A pretty idea is to lay masses of flowers on the ground where the tent meets the floor or grass.

If the wedding is indoors then much will depend on what sort of room the reception is held in. An unusual idea might be to hand each guest a highly scented rosebud as they greet the bride and groom. This will set the mood for a 'flowery' reception! You want to use fresh flowers in abundance both in formal displays but also as decorations for walls, windows and the wedding table where the wedding feast will take place. If you are using a series of small tables then design your colour scheme and carry this through, relating the flowers and colour scheme in subtle ways. For instance, many brides choose pink and white as their wedding colours, maybe dressing their bridesmaids in pink while they themselves wear white. This colour scheme can be matched throughout the room using different flowers in pink and white in large and small displays. Each table could be decked out in either pink or white with matching or contrasting flowers. Use all the highly scented flowers you can find in these colours: roses, pinks, carnations, lilies, magnolia, jasmine, honeysuckle and peonies. Perhaps all the men should be asked to wear white carnations in their buttonholes and all the ladies a pink rose! Ribbons should be used extravagantly. They are very festive for weddings and can be used on their own in big bows with flowing tails or with flowers in all kinds of displays.

The Wedding Table

If one large table is to be used then the decoration becomes easier. On a beautiful white cloth lay pale, scented sprays of flowers; float flowers in glass bowls of water; use fresh or crystallized flowers to stick on to place name cards. Lace napkins can be encircled with summer flowers and ribbons and each one can be different. You could place a small posy of fresh flowers beside each guest's plate so that they have something to take home with them after the festivities are over.

If the meal is a buffet one then the table can be garlanded with flowers that loop around the outside of the cloth. These may get crushed as guests move towards the food, but then they will smell the lovely scents of the flowers, so don't worry too much about this.

Perhaps for a very special flowery wedding you could have individual menus written out in beautiful script and decorated with crystallized flowers stuck on to them, or even a fresh rosebud secured to the top of each menu might be fun. Serve ice creams and sorbets in flower ice bowls for a really stunning effect (see p.119)

The Wedding Cake

Ask whoever is baking your cake to decorate it lavishly with fresh and crystallized flowers. The crystallized flowers can be stuck on all round the sides in attractive patterns with fresh sprays, in miniature, laid carefully on each layer.

BUFFET PARTY

Spiced Stuffed Eggs with marigolds, chervil and anchusa
Vegetable Platter
Fish and Flower Terrine
Ceviche with sage flowers
Tabbouleh with flowers

Chicken in melons with honeysuckle
Cold Seafood Pasta with chive flowers
Wholemeal red and yellow pepper quiche with pansies

Nasturtium salad
Watercress, apple, walnut and chrysanthemum salad
Fennel salad with pansies and pot marigolds
Perfumed petal salad
Rocket salad with heartsease and dandelions

Summer Fruit and Flower Jelly
Primavera salad with violets and exotic fruits
Flower Cookies
Stuffed Flower Oranges

Mint Flower Ice Cream
Sweet Geranium Ice Cream
Rose Petal Ice Cream
Redcurrant sorbet with thyme flowers
Exotic Lavender sorbet

The Buffet Party

Throughout the buffet party you can serve a summer punch scented with
rose petals (see page 135). You want to put the punch into a wide, glass
or china bowl, and make it look as pretty as possible by keeping it fresh
with flower petals and ice cubes.

A summer buffet party, providing the weather is good, can be the
most fun party of them all. You might have it in a tent or a conservatory
or in a room in your house. If it is really hot and you're sure the weather
will hold then there's nothing nicer than having it in the garden.

If you have an evening party in the garden make sure you light the
garden prettily. You can use outdoor lights, lanterns, flares or night-
lights set in saucers of water. Lights of any kind will make your garden,
and indeed any room, look romantic and welcoming.

For flower decorations the scope is unlimited. You can either decide to go for flowers on a grand scale and get someone in to do formal displays, or you can do your own, using whatever flowers there are in season. Try not to clutter a room and make sure that the flowers are where people who are enjoying themselves will not crash into them! I still think one of the nicest ways to decorate a room is to garland the walls. Here the flowers are out of the way and yet very visible and you can do most of the work the day before. Use wire, heavy cord or ribbons to make garlanded loops around the walls and then weave your flowers around these materials. Where each garland has to be pinned in a loop, secure these with ribboned bows and more flowers. Hang flowers from central lights too, providing they are not too low.

The Buffet Table

Here your priority must be to have enough space for the food. With this in mind, unless you have a vast table, it is best to keep the floral decorations to a small scale. Modest vases on stable bases filled with summer flowers and herbs will look lovely as a background for the food. If you are using honeysuckle for example in a certain dish then it might be nice to have a small vase of the flowers near the dish to complement it. Follow the colour schemes of the food in the flowers so the whole table has a unity about it. I always like to decorate the outside of the table. You can loop sprays of flowers on the cloth which will look gorgeously pretty and even if the guests crush them it won't matter because then they will get the benefits of the glorious scents of the flowers as they brush against them. Use highly scented flowers such as roses, honeysuckle, lavender, peonies, hyacinths, lilies, meadowsweet, mint, stocks, sweet woodruff, violets and thyme. Never worry about mixing the grand with the humble – a tiny violet will go very well with the most imposing peony!

If it is a very hot night you can make up some flower ice cubes which you can pile on the table for guests to hold to cool themselves down! To make these you fill an ice tray half full, add a scented flower like a rose petal, lavender, violet, floret of hyacinth or some herb flowers, then freeze. Fill up the ice tray and freeze again. Now you will have a pretty ice cube. You can put them in drinks too! Serve the ices and sorbets in flower ice bowls for a special effect (see page 119).

STARTERS

If you are going to serve a meal which includes flowers, you want your guests to be immediately excited by the idea of actually eating them! So, in your *Starters*, use as many brilliant and scented flowers as you can — but with discretion. Anyone will be seduced by the bright primroses with the avocado, and you can make your flower-bedecked vegetable platter into a beautiful picture.

Use the flowers as you mean to go on throughout the meal. Introduce your friends to the great variety of colours and scents that we are all familiar with in our gardens but have rarely seen on the dinner table!

A simple dish like scrambled eggs can be transformed by the addition of a colourful flower like borage. Anchusa, so often thought of as nothing more than a weed, makes an exotic accompaniment to artichoke hearts, giving them a brilliant appearance which will excite all those who eat them! Spring flowers like English cowslips and primroses have the perfect flavour for fish dishes, while sage and chive flowers have a more herby taste and look stunning with any dish.

AVOCADO PEAR WITH CRAB, PEAR, PEACH AND PRIMROSES

Serves 4

2 avocado pears
8oz/225g fresh crab meat
3-4 tablespoons Creamy vinaigrette (see page 61)
1 ripe pear
1 ripe peach
1 tablespoon freshly picked primroses, to garnish

Halve the avocados and remove the stones. Mix the crab meat with the vinaigrette and fill the avocados with this mixture.

Peel and slice the pear and peach and tuck slices of each into the crab meat. Decorate the avocados with fresh primroses and serve immediately with thin fingers of toast and butter.

CEVICHE WITH SAGE FLOWERS

Serves 4

Serve this sharp-tasting appetizer in a pretty white china bowl or china scallop shells, accompanied by Melba toast and butter.

4 plaice fillets, skinned
1 medium onion
1 fresh green chilli
juice 2—4 fresh limes
purple sage flowers, to garnish

Cut the plaice fillets into thin strips. Finely slice or chop the onion and slice the chilli into very thin rings, discarding all the seeds.

Arrange the fish in a bowl or individual dishes and scatter over the sliced or chopped onion and chilli. Pour over enough lime juice just to cover the fish and leave to marinate in the refrigerator for at least 4 hours. Decorate with sage flowers just before serving.

WHOLEMEAL RED AND YELLOW PEPPER QUICHE WITH PANSIES

Serves 6–8 as a starter, or 4–6 as a main dish

This colourful starter also makes a great supper or lunch dish served with new green peas or a leafy salad. Its bright colours make it appealing to both adults and children and it is very easy to make.

Pastry

8oz/225g (2 cups) wholemeal flour
pinch salt
4oz/100g (½ cup) sunflower margarine, cubed
4fl oz/125ml (½ cup) iced water
butter, for greasing
pinch flour

Filling

2oz/50g (¼ cup) butter or sunflower margarine
1 tablespoon sunflower oil
2 onions, very thinly sliced
½ red pepper, seeded and thinly sliced
½ yellow pepper, seeded and thinly sliced
3 tablespoons purple pansies
3 small or 2 large eggs
2oz/50g (½ cup) Cheddar or Gruyère cheese, grated
½pt/275ml (1¼ cups) milk
sea salt and black pepper

First make the flan case: sift the flour and salt into a large bowl and tip in the bran remaining in the sieve. Chop the margarine into the flour with a knife, then gently rub in with your fingertips until the mixture resembles fine breadcrumbs. Lift your fingers above the bowl as you rub to keep the mixture light and aerated. Add the iced water and mix in with a knife until you have a firm dough. Lift out the dough, wrap in cling film and chill in the fridge for 5–10 minutes.

Heat the oven to 350F/180C/gas 4.

On a lightly floured marble or wooden surface, roll out the chilled dough thinly into a circle large enough to line an 8–10-in/20–24cm flan dish. Grease the dish and line with the wholemeal dough. Set aside.

To make the filling, heat the butter and oil in a shallow pan, put in the onions and peppers and sweat gently until the vegetables are soft but not coloured. Add the pansies.

Whisk the eggs and stir in the grated cheese and milk. Season to taste. Pour the onion and pepper mixture into the egg mixture and stir well. Pour into the prepared flan case. Bake in the oven for 25–30 minutes, raising the heat a little if necessary, until the filling is nicely puffed up and the pastry is beginning to brown. Serve hot or cold.

CORN AND MARIGOLD FRITTERS

Serves 4

This is an excellent supper dish, which children will enjoy. Serve the fritters with a hot green vegetable or salad and brown bread and butter.

8oz/225g sweetcorn kernels (1 cup whole kernel corn)
4 tablespoons double (heavy) cream
1 tablespoon flour
1/2 teaspoon baking powder (baking soda)
sea salt and white pepper
1 tablespoon marigold petals*
1–2 tablespoons sunflower oil

Put the sweetcorn in a bowl and pour over the cream. Sift in the flour and baking powder (soda) and season to taste. Stir in the marigold petals.

Set a large, heavy frying pan over high heat and pour in 1 tablespoon oil. Drop spoonfuls of the fritter mixture into the oil and fry until golden on both sides, turning once. Press the mixture flat with a spatula to give a lacy effect at the edges.

Cook the fritters in batches until all the mixture is used up, adding more oil to the pan if necessary. Serve hot.

*Make certain that you use a pot marigold (*Calendula*) rather than an African marigold (*Tagetes*).

ARTICHOKE HEARTS WITH PRAWNS AND ANCHUSA

Serves 4

It is best to use canned artichoke hearts for this dish, which has a stunning appearance with the pale green of the artichokes, the pink prawns and the brilliant blue anchusa flowers. Serve in pretty glass dishes with a plate of Melba toast and rolled butter pats.

12 small canned artichoke hearts, drained
8oz/225g prawns (shrimps), peeled
5fl oz/150ml (⁵⁄₈ cup) soured cream
sprigs fresh dill, finely chopped
1 tablespoon anchusa flowers

Place 3 artichoke hearts in each dish, pile a few prawns (shrimps) on top of each one and spoon over the soured cream. Sprinkle some chopped dill over the top, then top with the anchusa flowers.

TABBOULEH WITH FLOWERS

Serves 4–6

Tabbouleh is a delicious bulgar (cracked) wheat salad which can be made extra special by serving it with tiny cornflower (Bachelor's button) petals. It makes a superb lunch dish with black olives and a green salad.

8oz/225g coarse bulgar wheat (1½ cups cracked wheat)
4oz/100g (1 cup) fresh parsley, chopped
1 large onion, chopped or 3–4 spring onions (scallions), chopped
4 tablespoons fresh mint, finely chopped
6 tablespoons olive or sunflower oil
4 tablespoons lemon juice
8oz/225g tomatoes, skinned, seeded and chopped
1 tablespoon cornflower petals
salt and pepper

Soak the bulgar (cracked) wheat for about 1 hour. Drain thoroughly in a sieve, pressing the water out with your hands. Spread the drained bulgar wheat on a clean cloth to allow to dry further.

In a large bowl, combine all the remaining ingredients. Mix in the bulgar wheat, adjust the seasoning and serve.

STUFFED WILD MUSHROOMS WITH LEMON, BAY AND DANDELION PETALS

Serves 4

Use large, flat wild mushrooms. Serve with garlic bread and, for a lunch or supper dish, a leafy green salad.

4 large or 8 medium flat wild mushrooms
2 tablespoons vegetable oil
1 small onion, finely chopped
1 garlic clove, crushed
4 tablespoons fresh breadcrumbs
1–2 tablespoons chopped parsley
twists lemon peel
fresh bay leaves
young dandelion leaves
sea salt and black pepper
fresh dandelion petals, to garnish

Remove the mushroom stalks, chop and reserve. Wipe the caps clean with a paper towel.

Heat half the oil in a frying pan, put in the onion, garlic, breadcrumbs and parsley and fry gently for 2–3 minutes, until the onion is soft. Carefully scoop out some of the mushroom flesh from the caps, using a small spoon, taking care not to damage the outer shell, and add it to the pan, together with the chopped stalks. Cook, stirring for 1–2 minutes.

Stuff the mushrooms with the mixture. Add the remaining oil to the pan, put in the stuffed mushrooms and fry gently for 3–4 minutes.

Arrange the lemon twists, bay leaves and dandelion leaves on a warmed dish and lay the mushrooms on top. Sprinkle over salt and pepper to taste and garnish with dandelion petals.

VEGETABLE PLATTER

This entrancingly simple dish is perfect for the buffet table. Arrange the cold, stuffed vegetables on a large platter and decorate it with lots of herbs and fresh flowers. Serve it to your guests in the garden as part of a buffet on a warm summer's evening.

Courgettes (Zucchini)

Top and tail the courgettes (zucchini) and cook them until they are just done but still crunchy. Halve them and, using a grapefruit spoon, hollow out the inside leaving a little of the flesh. Throw away the rest which will contain mostly seeds. Mash a little hard boiled egg with a few finely chopped spring onions (scallions) and some cornflower (Bachelor's button) petals. Bind the mixture together with good mayonnaise. Fill the courgettes (zucchini) with the mixture and decorate with fresh cornflower (Bachelor's button) petals.

Carrots

Take a few carrots of the same size and clean them. Boil or steam them until cooked but still crunchy. Halve the carrots and scoop out the inside, just as with the courgettes. Fill with some chopped cooked chicken, a little fresh tarragon and torn yellow pansies. Mix with a little mayonnaise and decorate with fresh pansy petals.

New Potatoes

Steam or boil some new potatoes in their skins until they are cooked. Peel them and cut in half. Scoop out a hollow in each half and fill with cottage cheese mixed with red bergamot flower petals or red rose petals. Decorate with fresh petals.

Mange-tout

Wash the mange-tout and cook for 1 minute in a little boiling salted water. Remove from the water and plunge straight away into very cold water. Drain well. Carefully slit open each pod and fill with a few delicate rosemary flowers or May or hawthorn blossoms.

SOUPS

The delicate flavours and scents of flowers go well with soups. Cooking the soup with the flowers imparts a subtle flavour, and a spectacular garnish of fresh flowers sprinkled on top just before serving adds an extra dimension to even the simplest of soups. Some flowers, like pot marigolds, have been traditionally used in soups and stews since the earliest times. Culpeper and Gerard, two of the great herbalists, both agree that marigolds in broth 'strengthen the heart exceedingly'. It is nice to think as you partake of your bowl of soup, that often you are eating flowers which have a medicinal value as well as a delicious taste.

You can also add herbs to soups but you should choose these carefully since they are stronger tasting than flowers and can drown their softer and gentler flavours. Sweet woodruff is a little-used flower and yet it has a lovely new-mown hay flavour and goes well in all kinds of soups. Use a few chopped leaves as well as the flowers, if you like, since the two together will give your soup a special flavour. To offset a rich vegetable like pumpkin, I have used sage flowers. These are particularly good in hearty soups and are also beneficial. Gerard, in his famous *Herball*, tells us that 'sage is singularly good for head and brain, the senses and memory....'

YOGURT AND MINT SOUP WITH MINT FLOWERS

Serves 3–4

This is definitely a soup for a summer's day, with its fresh, cooling, minty flavour and delectable green and white colours. Only make the soup if you have fresh mint; dried will not do for this recipe.

16fl oz/450ml (2 cups) Greek-style or thick yogurt
2 tablespoons chopped fresh mint leaves
3 tablespoons mint flowers
2in/5cm piece cucumber, sliced
sea salt and black pepper
4fl oz/125ml (½ cup) milk, optional
3–4 slices cucumber, to garnish
mint flowers, to garnish

Combine the yogurt, chopped mint leaves and flowers, cucumber and salt and pepper to taste in a blender or food processor and blend until smooth. Leave in the fridge for at least 2 hours for the flavours to develop.

Just before serving, thin the soup with a little milk. Serve in individual bowls, topped with a slice of cucumber and some pretty mauve mint flowers scattered over.

right: Summer salads and starters appeal to both the eye and the palate. The fish terrine is packed with flowers and is encased in a thin layer of sorrel (see pages 76–77); sharp and seductive ceviche is enhanced by sage flowers (see page 19); the bean salad is filling and pretty (see page 58), while the nasturtiums brilliantly set off the dark green watercress and white chicory leaves (see page 56).

overleaf: A delectable vegetable platter for the buffet table – courgettes (zucchini) stuffed with egg and cornflowers (Bachelor's buttons); carrots filled with cold chicken in mayonnaise with yellow pansies; crisp mange-tout with rosemary flowers, and new potatoes stuffed with cottage cheese and red bergamot flowers (see page 24).

PUMPKIN SOUP WITH SAGE FLOWERS

Serves 4–6

This hearty soup makes a good lunch dish, served with hot wholewheat garlic bread.

2 onions, chopped
3 garlic cloves, peeled and cut into slivers
1 tablespoon sunflower oil
3 tomatoes, skinned and chopped
1lb/450g pumpkin, peeled, sliced and seeds removed
1 tablespoon tomato paste
sea salt and black pepper
1½pt/850ml (3¾ cups) vegetable stock
3 sprigs flowering sage

Put the onions, garlic and oil in a heavy saucepan and heat gently for 3–4 minutes. Add the tomatoes and pumpkin, stir in the tomato paste and season to taste. Cook for 3–4 minutes, stirring continuously.

Add the stock, stir well and cook for a further 5–10 minutes, until the pumpkin is tender. Stir in most of the sage flowers, then purée the soup and serve garnished with fresh sage flowers.

previous page: The biggest occasion of all – the wedding – heralds a beautifully decorated floral cake which combines dried, crystallized, silk and fresh flowers in an imaginative and elegant way which will delight any bride and groom (see pages 13–15).

left: Herb and flower cheeses: Belle des Champs flavoured with thyme and fennel; pot marigolds and scented-leaved geraniums adorn a modest goat's cheese; Brie benefits from the decorative and highly scented leaves of lemon balm while cottage cheese is mixed with blue pansies and fresh watercress in a pot. Rosemary and nasturtium scent curd cheese; La Bouille is potted with torn carnation petals and salad burnet; and heartsease and watercress liven up another goat's cheese (see page 40).

CHILLED PINK CONSOMMÉ

Serves 4–6

This prettily coloured tomato soup is decorated with basil and sorrel flowers. Alice B. Toklas includes the basic recipe in her book *Aromas and Flavours of Past and Present*. I have added the herb flowers for a more unusual taste. The soup looks best served in white bowls.

3 large ripe tomatoes, skinned and chopped
2 large basil leaves, torn into pieces
2pt/1L(5 cups) chicken or vegetable stock
salt and pepper
4 tablespoons double (heavy) cream
basil and sorrel flowers, to decorate

Simmer the chopped tomatoes and basil leaves in the stock for 25 minutes. Season to taste, then strain through a sieve and leave to cool.

Serve the soup well chilled in individual bowls. Decorate each with a swirl of cream and a sprinkling of basil and sorrel flowers.

SORREL SOUP WITH SORREL FLOWERS AND SOURED CREAM

Serves 4–6

4oz/100g young sorrel leaves
1 large onion
1 large potato
1 tablespoon butter
1½pt/850ml (3¾ cups) chicken or vegetable stock
sea salt and black pepper
½pt/275ml (1¼ cups) milk
5fl oz/150ml (⅝ cup) soured cream
sorrel flowers, to decorate

Wash the sorrel leaves and discard the stalks. Roughly chop the onion and potato.

Melt the butter in a large, heavy pan and put in the sorrel, onion and potato. Sweat the vegetables over gentle heat, stirring occasionally, until they begin to soften. Pour in the stock, bring to the boil, then lower the heat and simmer gently for 25–30 minutes, until the vegetables are very soft.

Purée the soup in a food processor or blender, or rub through a mouli. Season to taste, then stir in enough milk to give the soup a good consistency.

Serve the soup in individual bowls, topped with a spoonful of soured cream and decorated with pretty sorrel flowers. Hot buttered toast and a little grated mature Cheddar cheese make a good accompaniment.

SPRING GREENS SOUP

Serves 4–6

Serve this delicate spring soup, with its lovely fresh green colour, dotted with English cowslips or primroses and accompanied by fingers of lightly fried wholewheat bread.

1 tablespoon butter
2 onions, chopped
3 potatoes, chopped
3 tablespoons young nettle tops, washed and dried
3 tablespoons young spinach leaves, washed and dried
3 tablespoons English cowslips or primroses
1 tablespoon flour
1½pt/850ml (3¾ cups) vegetable stock
salt and pepper
English cowslips or primroses, to garnish

Melt the butter in a large heavy pan, put in the onions and potatoes and sweat for 3–4 minutes. Add the nettle tops and spinach and cook for a further 3–4 minutes. Add the English cowslips or primroses and stir briskly.

Stir in the flour, then slowly pour in the stock, stirring continuously. Season to taste and bring the mixture slowly to the boil. Half cover the pan with a lid and simmer the soup for 1 hour. Purée in a blender or food processor, or pass through a mouli if you prefer a coarser texture. Sprinkle with English cowslips or primroses and serve at once.

CHERRY SOUP WITH SWEET WOODRUFF

Serves 4–6

This soup is one of my old favourites. You can make it with fresh or canned cherries and serve it either hot or cold. The sweet woodruff flowers add a new-mown hay taste and look very pretty.

2lb/900g fresh red cherries, stalks and stones removed
7fl oz/200ml (⅞ cup) red wine
2pt/1L (5 cups) water
2 tablespoons sweet woodruff flowers
1 cinnamon stick, broken into 3 pieces
sugar, to taste
1 teaspoon cornflour (cornstarch), optional
5fl oz/150ml (⅝ cup) natural yogurt
fresh sweet woodruff flowers, to decorate

In a large saucepan, combine the cherries, wine, water, half the woodruff flowers and the cinnamon. Bring to the boil, then lower the heat and simmer for 20–30 minutes, until the cherries are soft.

Remove the woodruff and cinnamon and purée the soup in a blender or food processor, adding a little sugar to taste, if necessary. If the soup is very thin, stir in the cornflour (cornstarch), return the soup to the saucepan and boil for about 2 minutes, until thickened.

Serve the soup hot or chilled and stir in a good dollop of yogurt just before serving. Decorate with the remaining sweet woodruff flowers.

Alternative quick recipe

Serves 4

A most unusual starter, with a pleasing taste and amazing purple colour.

1 × 15oz/425g can black cherries, stoned (pitted)
11fl oz/300ml (1⅜ cups) natural yogurt
¼ teaspoon ground cinnamon
1 tablespoon sweet woodruff flowers
sweet woodruff flowers, to decorate

Put all the ingredients into a blender or food processor and blend until smooth. Serve chilled, decorated with fresh sweet woodruff flowers.

CHESTNUT AND MUSHROOM SOUP WITH MARIGOLDS

Serves 4–6

This delicious, creamy winter soup is enhanced by the fragrance of marigold petals. If fresh petals are not available, dried will do perfectly well. The soup is very filling, so serve it for lunch on a cold winter day, or as an early starter on Christmas Day.

1lb/450g fresh chestnuts
2 tablespoons butter
1 onion, finely chopped
2 large, dark field mushrooms, peeled and finely sliced
5 fl oz/150ml (⅝ cup) vegetable or chicken stock
2 tablespoons fresh or dried marigold petals*
salt and pepper
15 fl oz/425ml (1⅞ cups) creamy milk
chopped parsley and marigold petals*, to serve

Simmer the chestnuts in water or stock for 15 minutes, until tender. Peel and set aside.

Heat the butter and sauté the chopped onion for 2 minutes, until soft but not coloured. Add the chestnuts and mushrooms and cook for a further 2–3 minutes. Add the stock and marigold petals and season lightly. Heat for 1 minute, then add the milk and cook until hot.

Purée the soup in a blender or food processor until almost, but not quite, smooth; you should still be able to see tiny pieces of chestnut and mushroom in the soup. Garnish with chopped parsley and marigold petals and serve hot.

*Make certain that you use a pot marigold (*Calendula*) rather than an African marigold (*Tagetes*).

CHEESE DISHES AND HERB AND FLOWER CHEESES

The often strong flavour of cheese can be nicely offset by using a variety of herbs, herb flowers and scented flowers. Pot marigolds and nasturtiums go particularly well with cheese dishes, as do sage flowers with their distinctive flavour. Violets are exceedingly good with hot melted cheese, adding a wonderful scent and colour. Use flowers as imaginatively as you can with cheeses, taking account of their different colours and flavours. Chive flowers, for instance, not only taste excellent with cheese dishes but their mauve florets look magnificent, too. All herb flowers go well with cheese dishes; you can also use the herbs themselves so that both flowers and leaves enhance the dish.

An imaginative way to serve soft cheeses is to flavour them with herbs and flowers; I have given suggestions for these on page 40. They make a delightful spread for a buffet party and are a lovely way to end a meal.

*Make certain that you use a pot marigold (*Calendula*) rather than an African marigold (*Tagetes*).

POT CURD CHEESE WITH CHERVIL, LOVAGE AND MARIGOLD PETALS

Serves 4

8oz/225g (1 cup) soft curd cheese
1 tablespoon chervil, chopped
1 tablespoon lovage, chopped
1 tablespoon marigold petals*, chopped
sea salt and black pepper
pinch freshly grated nutmeg
chopped fresh herbs and marigold petals*, to decorate

Beat the curd cheese with the chopped herbs and petals and season with salt, pepper and nutmeg. Press the mixture into small ramekins and decorate with fresh herbs and marigold petals. Cover and keep in the refrigerator until needed. Serve with a variety of wholewheat crackers or bread.

HOT GOAT'S CHEESE WITH PETAL TOMATOES

Serves 4

Serve this lovely peasanty dish on a bed of hot buttered spinach or sorrel, accompanied by home-made wholemeal bread.

4 small goat's cheeses, each weighing 3-4 oz/75–100g
½ teaspoon paprika
4 large tomatoes, halved
1 garlic clove, crushed
salt and pepper
1 tablespoon chopped chives
1 tablespoon basil leaves, chopped
chive and basil flowers, to garnish

Heat the grill to hot.

Sprinkle the cheeses with paprika. Spread the tomato halves with garlic, salt, pepper and the chives and basil, adding a few herb flowers. Grill the cheeses and tomatoes until hot, turning the cheeses once. Add a few more herb flowers to the tomatoes and serve at once.

CHEESE AND ONION HOT POT WITH MARIGOLDS, CHERVIL AND LOVAGE

Serves 4–6

Serve the hot pot with a green salad to which you have added chervil flowers and chopped parsley. Be careful not to overdo the herbs, especially the lovage, which has an extremely strong flavour and could be overpowering.

4 tablespoons butter
2 onions, thinly sliced
8 potatoes, thinly sliced
sea salt and black pepper
pinch grated nutmeg
pinch ground mace
1 tablespoon chopped chervil
1 teaspoon chopped lovage
1 tablespoon marigold petals*
4oz/100g (1 cup) Emmenthal, Gruyère or mature Cheddar cheese, grated
½pt/275ml (1 cup) milk

Heat the oven to 325F/170C/gas 3.

Butter a heavy earthenware casserole and put in alternate layers of sliced onions and potatoes, dotting each layer with a little butter, a mixture of salt, pepper, nutmeg and mace, a thin sprinkling of chervil, lovage and marigold petals and then a thick layer of grated cheese.

Continue to make layers in this way, finishing with a layer of potato. Dot with butter and sprinkle with nutmeg, then pour in enough milk to come about half-way up the side of the casserole. Top with grated cheese and bake in the oven for about 2 hours, or until the potatoes are soft. Serve immediately.

*Make certain that you use a pot marigold (Calendula) rather than an African marigold (Tagetes).

COLD CHEESE ALEXANDER

Serves 4

In her book *Aromas and Flavours of Past and Present*, Alice B. Toklas says that this dish is good with cockles or as an accompaniment to salad. She suggests eating it with 'fingers of rye bread lightly toasted but not buttered and served very hot as a contrast to the cold, cold cheese.' I suggest serving it with anchusa flowers.

4oz/100g (½ cup) butter, softened
4oz/100g (½ cup) Roquefort cheese, diced
½ teaspoon paprika
1 teaspoon chopped chives
4fl oz/125ml (½ cup) dry sherry
anchusa flowers, to garnish

Blend all the ingredients in a blender or food processor until smooth.

Line 4 small ramekins or pots with cling film and fill with the cheese mixture. Chill in the refrigerator for at least 1 hour, then turn out the moulds, remove the cling film and decorate with fresh comfrey flowers.

CHEESE RAREBIT WITH MUSTARD OR TANSY FLOWERS

Serves 4

The flowers give this old favourite a very special and unique flavour. Serve the rarebit as a snack for lunch, with a crisp green salad.

4 thick slices wholewheat bread
2 tablespoons butter
2 tablespoons wholegrain mustard
4oz/100g (1 cup) strong Cheddar cheese, grated
tansy or mustard flowers, to taste

Heat the grill to high.

Lightly toast the bread on both sides, then, while it is still hot, butter each slice and spread with a good layer of mustard. Spread over the grated cheese and sprinkle on a few flowers.

Toast under the grill until the cheese is bubbling and serve at once.

CHEESE, FRUIT AND FLOWER APPETIZER

Serve this refreshing starter with crisp wholewheat toast.

In a serving bowl, combine small cubes of feta cheese, slices of crisp apple with the skin left on, orange segments, sliced banana and halved and seeded black and green grapes. Add lemon juice to taste and toss well. Stir in a tiny quantity of sunflower oil (the exact amount will depend on how much fruit and cheese you have used). Just before serving, add some violets, rose petals and pot marigold petals.

HERB AND FLOWER CHEESES

A lovely way to start a summer's lunch in the garden is to lay out on a wooden board a variety of soft cheeses stuffed and rolled in herbs and flowers. They look spectacular and taste wonderful! You can serve these with lots of different wheaten biscuits and slabs of farmhouse butter, or sunflower margarine for the more health conscious.

You can use any soft cheeses. Shape into balls, slabs, round pats and oval shapes and roll in finely chopped flower petals and herbs, then lay the cheeses on fresh herbs garnished with flowers for the final presentation.

Cream cheese, cottage cheese, goat's cheese, blue cheese, curd cheese, Brie with the rind removed and several other softish French cheeses like Belle des Champs are all easily kneaded into different shapes and respond well to the tasty flavour of herbs and flowers.

Make round blue cheese balls covered with marjoram leaves and flowers; goat's cheese rolled in pot marigold petals or nasturtiums; cottage cheese (squeezed to remove all water) patted into round shapes and covered with chives and chive flowers and curd cheese spread in pots and covered with blue sage flowers. Brie and other soft cheeses can also be used in imaginative ways; slice and sandwich them together with a layer of thyme flowers and decorate with thyme herb and flowers. Lovage is a good herb to use with cheese; chop a little with a quantity of mallow flowers and use to cover small rounds of cheese.

You can make a really colourful arrangement of these various flower and herb cheeses and serve them in the garden or after dessert for supper. They also make a perfect buffet party dish. Your guests are bound to be delighted.

EGG DISHES

Eggs are a rich source of protein and can be nicely balanced in cooking by the use of various flowers of different flavours. Chive flowers, chervil and chervil flowers and real French tarragon all go well with egg dishes. You can decorate coddled eggs with the bright blue flowers of anchusa or deep purple violets while the tiny, delicate heartsease adds its own special scent and looks incredibly pretty.

Sprinkle herbs over all kinds of egg dishes and try matching up the flavour of the herbs with those of the flowers. Herb flowers like basil, thyme, marjoram and chervil are exceptionally good with eggs.

The multi-flower omelette (page 44) is a winner, leaving you to use your imagination to the full by incorporating in the omelette a gorgeous variety of your favourite garden flowers. Make this a scented delight which will certainly entice even the most sceptical of friends! Courgette (zucchini) and squash flowers are a 'must' in any flower cooking. They have a superb flavour and can be cooked in a variety of ways. Use them for decorating cold dishes for the buffet, too. They go exceptionally well with eggs.

SCRAMBLED EGGS WITH TARRAGON AND BORAGE FLOWERS IN PITTA

Serves 1

A delicious 'fun' lunch dish which children will enjoy.

1 tablespoon butter
2 eggs
salt and pepper
1 teaspoon fresh tarragon, finely chopped
1 spring onion (scallion), finely sliced
1 pitta bread
borage flowers, to decorate

Melt half the butter in a heavy pan set over low heat. Beat the eggs with salt and pepper to taste, the tarragon and spring onion (scallion). Pour the eggs into the pan and scramble with a wooden spoon, adding the remaining butter as they begin to cook.

Meanwhile, heat the pitta in the oven for a few minutes, then split in half widthways and fill each half with the scrambled eggs. Decorate with a few borage flowers and serve at once.

EGGS IN A POT WITH CHIVE AND MARIGOLD FLOWERS

Serves 4

I have modified Alice B. Toklas's charming recipe for soft-shelled eggs (from *Aromas and Flavours of Past and Present*). The chive and marigold flowers add extra flavour and look so pretty.

4 large eggs
butter, for greasing
4 tablespoons double (heavy) cream
salt and pepper
pinch nutmeg
2 tablespoons chopped chives
2 tablespoons marigold petals*
2 tablespoons chive flowers

Bring a pan of water to the boil, then put in the eggs and keep the water at a simmer. Cook the eggs for 4 minutes exactly, then put them under cold running water to ensure that the shells can be removed easily. Carefully shell the eggs and put them in a buttered dish or individual ramekins.

In a small pan, heat the cream with the seasonings until just warm. If you like, whip it lightly. Spoon it over the eggs and sprinkle with the chives and flowers and serve immediately with thinly sliced wholemeal bread and butter.

SPICED STUFFED EGGS WITH CHERVIL AND ANCHUSA

Serves 4

This makes an excellent buffet dish (just increase the quantities) and looks seductive on a bed of lacy cow parsley with the bright blue anchusa flowers topping each egg.

4 eggs
2 tablespoons home-made Mayonnaise (see page 62)
1 tablespoon chopped chervil
mild curry powder, to taste
1 tablespoon anchusa flowers, chopped
4 whole anchusa flowers, to decorate

Hard boil the eggs, place under running water for 2 minutes, then shell them.

Cut the eggs in half, put the yolks in a bowl and mash them with the mayonnaise, chervil, curry powder to taste and the chopped anchusa flowers. Fill the egg whites with a spoonful of this mixture, piling it up carefully. Place a single anchusa flower on top of each egg and serve on a platter decorated with cow parsley and other fresh herbs.

*Make certain that you use a pot marigold (*Calendula*) rather than an African marigold (*Tagetes*).

HANGOVER REMEDY!

Feeling jaded after a heavy night? Drink this remedy slowly, then lie on the floor and do some deep breathing exercises from your diaphragm. Rest for 1 hour – you're bound to feel better.

1 egg
2–3 drops light soy sauce
pinch lavender flowers

Break the egg into a glass and whisk until frothy. Add the soy sauce, then crush the lavender flowers in a pestle and mortar and add to the mixture. Liquidize, pour back into the glass and sip slowly.

MULTI-FLOWER OMELETTE

Serves 1

Use a mixture of your favourite garden flowers for this recipe – nasturtiums, pot marigolds, roses, thyme flowers, honeysuckle and mallows are all good. Let your imagination run riot and create your own mixture.

2 tablespoons mixed flowers
2 eggs
sea salt and black pepper
1 teaspoon vegetable oil

In a bowl, beat together the flowers and eggs and season to taste.

Heat the oil in an omelette pan and pour in the mixture. Cook quickly until the underside of the omelette is golden brown, then turn it over and cook the other side until golden, or sprinkle the top with more flowers if you like and fold over the omelette so that the centre is still soft.

VEGETABLE DISHES

Vegetables, with their different colours and textures, are ideal to serve and cook with flowers. Herb flowers go especially well with a variety of vegetables and their delicate scents and hues complement the blander-tasting vegetables.

A buttery dish of julienne of carrots can be transformed by the addition of tiny, purple marjoram flowers or brilliant heartsease. Mange-tout are perfect with spring primroses while courgettes (zucchini) can be given new life using rosemary flowers as a garnish. Chickweed is a useful flower to put with vegetables and is very good with buttered new potatoes.

You can really let your imagination fly with flowers and combined with vegetables the variation in colour is staggering. Choose vegetables which will contrast both in colour and taste with flowers and each dish will become a talking point. Treat your guests not only to dishes that taste superb but to a feast of visual delights which you, as the artist, have painted for them.

HOT CAULIFLOWER BAKE WITH CHEESE AND VIOLAS

Serves 4–6

1 cauliflower
2 tablespoons butter or sunflower margarine
1–2 tablespoons flour
4 fl oz/125ml (1/2 cup) milk
salt and pepper
pinch ground mace
freshly grated nutmeg
2–3oz/50–75g (1/2–3/4 cup) Gruyère cheese, grated
2 tablespoons finely chopped parsley
1 tablespoon viola petals
chopped parsley and fresh violas, to serve

Cook the cauliflower in plenty of boiling, salted water until just cooked but still crunchy. Drain, reserving about 1/4pt/150ml (5/8 cup) water. Separate the cauliflower florets and keep warm in an ovenproof dish.

Heat the oven to 375F/190C/gas 5.

In a saucepan, melt the butter and stir in enough flour to absorb all the butter. Cook gently for 1 minute, then stir in the reserved cauliflower water and the milk. Bring to the boil, stirring continuously, simmer for 2 minutes and season with salt, pepper, a little mace and plenty of nutmeg. Stir in half the cheese, the parsley and viola petals.

Pour the sauce over the cauliflower and sprinkle the remaining cheese over the top. Bake in the oven for about 25 minutes. Serve garnished with fresh parsley and violas.

right: A deliciously seductive summer table offers chilled melon filled with chicken and honeysuckle (see page 85) and spicy, curried flower eggs lying on a bed of lacy cow parsley and garnished with blue anchusa flowers (see page 43).

overleaf: A plate of stuffed courgette flowers makes a beautiful picture for the dinner table. They are filled with rice, nuts, dried fruits, fish or meat – all delicious in their own right (see page 53).

PUMPKIN, TOMATO, ONION AND NASTURTIUM BAKE

Serves 4

This is a really tasty dish which can be eaten on its own or with fish or white meats. If you like, garnish it with a few fresh nasturtium flowers just before serving – the dish will glow with the glorious colours of red, yellow and orange.

1–2 tablespoons sunflower oil
1lb/450g pumpkin, peeled, deseeded and sliced
2 onions, finely chopped
2 large tomatoes, skinned and sliced
3 tablespoons nasturtiums
salt and pepper
large pinch ground allspice

Heat the oven to 350F/180C/gas 4.

Lightly oil a shallow ovenproof dish and set aside. Heat the remaining oil in a frying pan, put in the pumpkin slices and fry gently for 3–4 minutes until lightly browned. With a slotted spoon, transfer the pumpkin to the prepared dish.

Put the onions in the frying pan and cook for about 2 minutes until soft but not brown. Add the sliced tomatoes and cook for 1 minute. Place the onions and tomatoes in the dish with the pumpkin, add the nasturtiums, season and sprinkle with allspice. Bake in the oven for about 30 minutes and serve hot.

previous page: Fresh and inspired spring dishes – fillets of plaice stuffed with English cowslips or chive flowers, lettuce hearts and chives (see page 75); mange-tout with primroses and chicory salad with heartsease (see page 59).

left: Flower vinegars and oils can conjure up summer scents in winter so make them throughout the summer months using highly perfumed flowers for the best results (see pages 64–65). left to right, nasturtium vinegar, marjoram flower oil, basil flower oil and lavender vinegar.

RED CABBAGE WITH APPLES AND CHRYSANTHEMUMS

Serves 4–6

This rich vegetable dish is excellent with pork and game.

1 red cabbage, cored and thinly sliced
2oz/50g (¼ cup) butter
1 large onion, sliced into rings
2 large cooking apples, peeled, cored and thickly sliced
2 tablespoons yellow chrysanthemum petals
2 tablespoons very dark brown sugar
5 tablespoons cold water
4 tablespoons red wine vinegar
sea salt and black pepper
butter and fresh chrysanthemum petals, to serve

Blanch the red cabbage in boiling water for 1 minute. Drain, refresh and set aside.

Heat the butter in a frying pan, put in the onion rings and sweat for 3–4 minutes, until soft. Stir in the apple slices and cook for 1 further minute.

Put the cabbage into a deep flameproof casserole with a tightly-fitting lid. Mix in the onion, apples and chrysanthemum petals and turn all the ingredients so that they become well coated with the butter. Sprinkle over the sugar and pour in the water and vinegar. Season lightly.

Cook over low heat, or in the oven at 325F/170C/gas 3, for 1½–2 hours, until the cabbage is soft. Just before serving, add a good knob of butter and some fresh chrysanthemum petals.

WHOLE STUFFED COURGETTE (ZUCCHINI) FLOWERS

Stuffed courgette (zucchini) flowers are very popular in Provence. The flowers can be stuffed with either cold fillings made from cooked rice, nuts, dried fruit, fish or meat bound together with mayonnaise – or any hot filling, in which case, lightly fry the stuffed flowers in a little oil just before serving.

A traditional Provençal method of serving the stuffed flowers is to bake them in tomato sauce. Serve the hot courgette (zucchini) flowers on a bed of buttered spinach or sorrel; cold ones may be served on a bed of fresh herbs.

When you pick the flowers for stuffing, make sure that they are dry and fully opened; clean them well before stuffing and beware of any insects which may be lurking in their depths!

CELERIAC PURÉE WITH PEARS OR QUINCES AND PELARGONIUMS

Serves 4

Choose the smoothest celeriac you can find; the knobblier they are, the harder they are to peel and you will get less edible vegetable for your money!

1lb/450g celeriac
lemon juice
2 tablespoons butter or *sunflower margarine*
salt
1 tablespoon pelargonium (scented-leaved geranium) flowers
2–4 pears or *quinces, peeled and sliced, to serve*
fresh pelargonium flowers, to decorate

Quarter the celeriac and peel it. Drop immediately into acidulated water (i.e. water with lemon juice or vinegar added) to prevent discoloration. Cut into cubes and boil or steam until tender, then rub through a mouli or sieve.

Mix in the butter, a little salt and the pelargonium flowers. Serve on a round platter surrounded by the sliced pears or quinces and sprinkled with more flowers.

BAKED POTATOES WITH WATERCRESS AND MARIGOLDS

Serves 4

Serve these potatoes with a multi-coloured salad of red, yellow and green peppers, garnished with sliced sweet onions and small purple pansies.

4 large baked potatoes
4 tablespoons butter
4–8 tablespoons cottage cheese
4 tablespoons watercress, chopped
2 tablespoons fresh marigold petals*
salt and pepper

Split the baked potatoes and fill each with a tablespoon of butter. Mix the cottage cheese with the watercress and marigold petals and put a good dollop of the mixture into each potato. Season to taste and serve with a multi-coloured pepper salad.

ROAST PARSNIPS WITH HONEY AND THYME FLOWERS

Serves 4

Eat these glorious rich brown parsnips with any meat dishes.

1lb/450g parsnips, trimmed and peeled
1–2 tablespoons clear honey
1 tablespoon sunflower oil
3–4 tablespoons thyme flowers

Heat the oven to 375F/190C/gas 5.

Brush the parsnips with a mixture of honey and oil and cover with thyme flowers. Place in a baking dish and bake in the oven, basting frequently, for about 1 hour, until deep golden brown. Sprinkle with fresh thyme flowers and serve at once.

*Make certain that you use a pot marigold (*Calendula*) rather than an African marigold (*Tagetes*).

SALADS AND SALAD DRESSINGS

The riotous colours of flowers really come into their own in salads. The brilliant colours and scents of flowers go exceptionally well with all kinds of salad greens and the combinations can be quite stunning. Try, for instance, tossing the scarlet, orange and yellow flowers of nasturtium into a bowl of herbs and salad greens. The result is superb. The peppery taste of the nasturtiums goes well with any kind of lettuce or cress and it will quickly become everyone's favourite.

Seafood and fish salads are especially good with flowers of all kinds. Try using chive flowers, pansies, mallow, dandelions and violets. For a sweet salad, rose petals are the obvious answer. Their delicious scent pervades everything and a delicate salad, perhaps made from a mixture of white and green leaves, can be delightfully enhanced by the addition of highly-scented rose petals or buds. Chrysanthemums are excellent in salads too, as are borage, pot marigolds and chickweed. Use blossoms like lime, elderflower, broom and red clover, which are all exceptionally adaptable to salads of all kinds.

SPINACH, BACON AND LILY SALAD

Cook some young spinach leaves for 1 minute, drain and dry. Arrange the crunchy spinach in a shallow earthenware bowl. Fry some green-back (unsmoked) bacon until very crisp. Drain on kitchen paper and crumble over the spinach. Toss the salad in a little sharp vinaigrette and finally add the torn petals of several Tiger lilies.

NASTURTIUM SALAD WITH YOUNG, FRESH SALAD LEAVES

In a large glass bowl combine lots of different green leaves, lettuce, dandelion (the young leaves only), sorrel, rocket and salad burnet. It is also quite a good idea to put in some young white chicory leaves for contrast. Add about 6 large nasturtium leaves and dress the salad in walnut vinaigrette (see page 61). Just before serving toss in about 12 brightly coloured nasturtium flowers. It will make a stunning looking salad and taste unusual and delicious.

SALAMAGUNDY

Hannah Glasse in her book *The Art of Cooking Made Plain and Easy* gives this very old recipe which is delightful and amazing in its variety. Salads in Hannah Glasse's day were not just made up of a few lettuce leaves but contained fish and meat and many different herbs and vegetables. They were meals in themselves and salamagundy is indeed a meal!

Use some or all of the following ingredients: minced cooked pork or veal, pickled herring, cucumber, apples, onions, pickled red cabbage, parsley, celery, cold duck or chicken, hard boiled eggs.

Butter the outside of a basin and put it upturned in the middle of a large dish. Lay around the edge and over the sides and top of the basin rings of the different ingredients to form a mound of cold meats and salads. Surround it with pickles, sliced lemons and lots of nasturtium leaves and flowers. You can add all kinds of herb flowers as well – try mint, lavender, marjoram and thyme. Make this salad the centrepiece of a cold buffet. It will certainly bring lots of comments!

RED CLOVER SALAD

Arrange some cooked rice in a bowl with slices of cucumber. Add a little chopped watercress, some cooked chicken or fish, a few slices of spring onions (scallions) and a small handful of pine nuts. Dress with home-made mayonnaise (see page 62) and add a quantity of red clover blossoms just before eating.

GRAPEFRUIT AND PRAWN SALAD WITH FENNEL AND ANCHUSA FLOWERS

Cut some grapefruit in half and carefully cut out all the segments leaving behind the rough skin. Scoop out all the skin and leave the grapefruit halves quite clean. Turn them upside down to drain. Shell about 2oz/50g of prawns or shrimps for each grapefruit half. Combine the grapefruit segments with the prawns in a little home-made mayonnaise (see page 62), mixed with a tiny spoonful of tomato purée and a spoonful of horseradish sauce. Add some chopped fresh fennel and put the mixture back into the grapefruit halves. Chill and decorate with bright blue flowers and serve immediately with crispy Melba toast.

SCENTED GREEN SALAD WITH VIOLETS

Combine the leaves of different kinds of sweet-scented geraniums with some lemon balm in a bowl and toss in a little dressing made from sunflower oil and lemon juice. Just before serving add a good bunch of Parma violets with the stalks and white heels removed from the petals. This salad gives off a wonderfully heady perfume and is quite unlike any other.

RED AND YELLOW PEPPER SALAD WITH BORAGE FLOWERS

Thinly slice one red and one yellow pepper into rings, discarding the pith and seeds. Lay the rings in a shallow salad bowl and add some sliced spring onions (scallions). Toss in a sharp vinaigrette made with dry mustard, lemon juice, corn oil, crushed garlic and white wine vinegar. Add a handful of blue borage flowers at the last minute.

WHITE BEAN SALAD WITH BORAGE FLOWERS

In a round, earthenware dish put some cooked haricot beans. Add green and red peppers cut into thin slivers. Chop a few fresh chives into one-inch pieces, tear some basil leaves and chop up a sprig or two of summer savoury and add these. Dress the salad with a sharp vinaigrette dressing flavoured with dry or wholegrain mustard. Finally throw in a handful of delicate borage flowers.

Serve this colourful and filling salad as a lunch dish or as a side dish for a cold repast. You can add fish, such as tuna or anchovy, if you like.

FRESH CRAB SALAD WITH MARIGOLDS

In a shallow bowl lay some crisp lettuce hearts. Add a sprig or two of fennel and tarragon bunched together. Place some lemon balm leaves on the other side of the dish. Combine fresh crab meat with a few prawns or shrimps and mix in home-made mayonnaise (see page 62). Place the shellfish in the centre of the lettuce. Slice a few radishes and decorate with these and some cucumber slices spread in a fan on either side of the dish. Sprinkle over the whole dish some fresh pot marigold petals and serve with slices of wholemeal bread and butter or hot wheaten rolls.

WATERCRESS, APPLE, WALNUT AND CHRYSANTHEMUM SALAD

Combine a bunch of freshly picked and washed watercress with slices of apple, lots of shelled walnuts and a quantity of dark yellow chrysanthemum petals which have been blanched and dried. Dress with a walnut vinaigrette (see page 61) and eat with hot, crisp French bread.

FENNEL SALAD WITH PANSIES AND MARIGOLDS

Slice a fennel bulb into thin rings and toss in vinaigrette. Add a handful of freshly picked pansies and lots of pot marigold petals. This makes a flavoursome side salad and goes well with fish.

PERFUMED PETAL SALAD WITH FRUIT SLICES

In a shallow glass dish which has been sprinkled with rose water put alternate layers of all kinds of edible flowers and petals – rose petals, rose buds, marigolds, sweet-scented geranium leaves and petals, borage flowers, honeysuckle, jasmine, sweet woodruff, lavender, thyme and mint, with slices of fresh fruit – oranges, apples, green and black grapes, pineapple, pears, kiwi fruit, pomegranates and banana. When the bowl is nearly full cover with a light, lemon-flavoured sugar syrup and a little white wine. Chill for an hour or so and then serve on Salad Bowl lettuce with a little cottage cheese.

CHICORY SALAD WITH HEARTSEASE

The tiny, fragrant pansies called heartsease look quite stunning in this green and white salad. If you can't get heartsease use violas instead.

Combine the white leaves of chicory with a good handful of watercress. Sprinkle over some chopped parsley and dress lightly in sunflower oil and lemon juice. Toss in a handful of heartsease and serve immediately.

ITALIAN TOMATO SALAD WITH SPRING ONIONS (SCALLIONS), BASIL AND ROSEMARY FLOWERS

Slice large, firm Italian tomatoes and chop some spring onions (scallions), scattering them over the tomatoes. Tear 4 large basil leaves and mix them with the onions and tomatoes. Add as many basil and rosemary flowers as possible. Sprinkle with sea salt and a very little olive oil, lemon juice and freshly milled black pepper. Eat at once.

MANGE-TOUT WITH PRIMROSES

Cook the mange-tout for 1–2 minutes, until they are tender but still crunchy. Drain and immediately plunge into iced water. Drain again and dry. Serve dressed with lemon juice and sunflower oil scattered with freshly picked primroses for a delicate and refreshing spring salad.

DANDELION SALAD WITH LEAVES AND PETALS AND BORAGE FLOWERS

Pick the young leaves of dandelions and some whole heads of flowers. Arrange the washed leaves in a glass bowl and tear the petals off the flower heads. Put in a few tiny lettuce hearts and several borage flowers. Dress with a thin yogurt dressing or a light vinaigrette.

ROCKET, PURSLANE, RADISH AND ANCHUSA SALAD

In a shallow white bowl, put a crushed clove of garlic. Slice some crisp radishes and add these. Sprinkle over a little sea salt. Add the young leaves of purslane and rocket. Toss in a little olive oil and lemon juice, add lots of anchusa flowers and serve immediately.

COWSLIPS, PRIMROSES AND HEARTSEASE WITH YOUNG SORREL AND ENDIVE

Spread some curly endive leaves in a shallow bowl and add a few young sorrel leaves and lots of English cowslips or primroses and heartsease (or violets). Eat without any dressing with wholemeal bread or pitta.

CHRYSANTHEMUM SALAD

Mrs Leyel in *The Gentle Art of Cooking* describes a chrysanthemum salad using 20 chrysanthemum flowers blanched in acidulated (i.e. water with lemon juice or vinegar added) and salted water, then drained and dried. She prefers to use dark yellow chrysanthemums. She mixes them with cold potatoes, artichoke hearts, shrimps' tails and capers in vinegar and decorates with hard boiled eggs and slices of beetroot and a pinch of saffron. You can use all these ingredients, possibly adding a few black olives and laying the salad on curly endive or lambs' lettuce. Whatever you use chrysanthemums have their own special taste which is quite unforgettable.

VINAIGRETTE

Makes about 6 fl oz/175ml (¾ cup)

2 teaspoons sugar (white or brown)
½ teaspoon dry mustard
1 garlic clove, crushed
3 tablespoons white wine vinegar or *lemon juice*
9 tablespoons olive oil and sunflower oil mixed

Put all the ingredients in a screw-top jar and shake vigorously. If you are not going to use all the vinaigrette straight away, it will keep very well in the jar. Shake well each time before using. For a more flowery vinaigrette, either add flowers just before using, or make the dressing with one of the flower vinegars on pages 64–65.

BLUE VINAIGRETTE

This is made by steeping deep purple, scented violet petals in a light wine vinegar for about 4 weeks. Stand the jar or bottle of vinegar and violets in the sun so that all the oils will be released from the flowers. Parma violets are good for this dressing and can easily be obtained by most florists when in season. This vinegar makes a lovely dressing for white salad leaves such as chicory, and for white fish salads.

Once the vinegar has obtained a good 'blue' colour, use it to make a blue vinaigrette as in the recipe above.

CREAMY VINAIGRETTE

This is excellent eaten with avocados stuffed with seafood and any cold fish or vegetables. To 6 tablespoons vinaigrette dressing, add 3 tablespoons double (heavy) cream and beat well together. Use this dressing immediately, because it will not keep.

WALNUT AND HAZELNUT VINAIGRETTE

The really delicious flavour of hazelnuts and walnuts will enhance any salad. Substitute these exotic nut oils for the olive and sunflower oils in the basic vinaigrette dressing.

MAYONNAISE

Home-made mayonnaise is always better than any commercial dressing bought in shops. Lots of people have a horror of making it thinking that it will curdle immediately! However, if you take care and time, making mayonnaise is terribly easy.

It is important to have all the ingredients at room temperature before you begin to make the mayonnaise.

Makes about ½pt/275ml (1¼ cups)

2 egg yolks
pinch salt
white pepper (optional)
½pt/275ml (1¼ cups) extra virgin olive oil
2 teaspoons lemon juice or white wine vinegar

Put the egg yolks into the clean, dry bowl of an electric mixer or blender and whisk them lightly. Add a pinch of salt and a very small amount of white pepper, if you like. Start pouring in the olive oil very, very gradually, beating all the time; as the mayonnaise thickens, you can add the oil more quickly. When it is quite thick, add the lemon juice or vinegar and then more oil. Taste it to see if it is to your liking; you may want to add more lemon juice or vinegar if you prefer a sharper flavour.

GREEN MAYONNAISE

This is my favourite dressing to eat with cold fish, especially salmon or salmon trout.

Make the mayonnaise as above. Chop a good bunch of watercress with some leaves of young sorrel and spinach and a few sprigs of real French tarragon. Blanch the green leaves in boiling water, refresh and dry well.

Pulverize the green leaves with a pestle and mortar and add a couple of teaspoons of anchusa flowers at this stage if you like. Add the almost puréed herbs and flowers to the mayonnaise and mix well together. It looks quite wonderful – green and speckled, with a little mauve showing through here and there if you have used the anchusa flowers.

Dress the fish with the mayonnaise and dot all over with fresh anchusa flowers.

CHINESE SWEET AND SOUR DRESSING

I have used this unusual dressing (one of Joy Larkcom's) with bean salads as well as with crunchy Chinese leaves and chicory. Make a syrup by warming 1 tablespoon sugar in a little water. Add the juice of a lemon and a little salt until your preferred sweet/sour balance is obtained. Mix with some soy sauce, a tablespoon of sesame oil, a tablespoon of wine vinegar, a little sliced fresh ginger root and a pinch of sugar.

SOUR CREAM DRESSING

Joy Larkcom uses this lovely dressing in her book *The Salad Garden*. It is useful for all kinds of salads and goes well with lettuce, herbs, flowers and bean salads. Mix ½pt/275ml (1¼ cups) sour cream with ½ teaspoon celery seed. Slowly stir in 1 tablespoon lemon juice or wine vinegar.

BLUE CHEESE DRESSING

8fl oz/225ml (1 cup) low fat yogurt
2oz/50g (¼ cup) any blue cheese, crumbled
2 spring onions (scallions), very finely chopped
2 teaspoons fresh parsley, finely chopped
2 teaspoons violets, finely chopped
2 tablespoons white wine vinegar
sea salt and freshly ground black pepper

Mix all the ingredients together and use immediately. This is an excellent dressing for cold pasta and cooked vegetables. It also goes very well with very crisp cos (romaine) lettuce and shredded cabbage salads.

ROSE SYRUP FOR FRUIT AND FLOWER SALADS

Steep 2 handfuls of highly scented rose petals in 1pt/575ml (2½ cups) very hot water for about an hour, then strain. Make a syrup by boiling the strained rose water with 1lb/450g (2 cups) sugar, making sure the sugar has dissolved completely before the liquid reaches boiling point. Boil for about 4 minutes. This syrup can be used for dressing fruit and flower salads or mixed with a little vinaigrette for a sweet/sour dressing.

FLOWER MUSTARDS, VINEGARS AND OILS

MUSTARDS

You can make lots of different flower mustards by chopping up fresh petals in wholegrain, hot English or spicy French mustards. These make unusual and pretty accompaniments for a variety of meat and fish dishes. It is best to use quite strong-tasting flowers with mustards so that their flavour will be bold enough to permeate the mustard.

Serve these flower mustards in tiny glass pots so that their charming appearance will be noticed by everyone at the table. Nothing looks prettier than wholegrain mustard with flecks of purple lavender in it or a smooth English mustard suffused with brilliant nasturtiums. You can use your imagination here and combine flowers that will complement your fish or meat dishes; for instance, mix mint flowers in a spicy French mustard to eat with pork and ham, sage flowers in smooth English mustard as a foil to a hearty breakfast of grilled bacon and tomatoes, or tiny fragrant dill flowers made into a sauce with wholegrain mustard to serve with substantial fish dishes.

Mustards can change their appearance dramatically with the addition of flowers, so experiment and see what you come up with.

Useful flowers to blend with mustards:
sage, nasturtiums, pot marigolds, red clover blossoms, dandelions, anchusa, lavender, pansies, thyme, mint, chervil, dill, fennel, hollyhocks and mallows.

VINEGARS

Unusual salads made with scented flower vinegars are delicious. The vinegars look pretty too, often taking on the colour of the flowers which are steeped in them, like rose petals, violets or lavender. It is best to use a good white wine vinegar for most flowers and a cider vinegar for darker ones like violets or deep red rose petals. To make the vinegar, steep any highly scented flowers in it for about 3–4 weeks, leaving the glass jar or bottle to stand on a sunny windowsill. In this way the sun will release the natural oils of the flowers which will impart their beautiful flavour to the vinegar.

Remove all stalks, green parts and the white heels of petals before using the flowers. For sprigs of lavender you can use an ordinary wine or vinegar bottle, but for petals it is best to put them in wide-necked jars and cover with a cork or cling film. Pack the flowers well down in the jar, then pour over the vinegar. Give the flowers a good stir before you seal the jar. You can shake the vinegar once each day to ensure that the petals or buds are thoroughly stirred up in the vinegar.

Suitable flowers to use for flower vinegars are:

violets, elderflowers, nasturtiums, lavender, rosemary, thyme, basil, roses, carnations, mint, primroses, pelargoniums and English cowslips.

When using a flower vinegar for a salad dressing make sure that you use a very light oil, like sunflower, so that it will not drown the delicately scented flower flavour.

OILS

Flower oils are full of flavour and when used in a winter salad or pasta dish conjure up the aroma of summer. Scented flowers go well with light oils, such as sunflower, while strong-smelling herb flowers can take a rich oil like olive, walnut or hazelnut.

Choose either a wide-necked jar or bottle, preferably an attractive glass one, put in a handful or two of flowers or a sprig of flowering herb and fill the bottle to the top with sunflower, olive, hazelnut or walnut oil. Cork the jar or bottle and leave in the sunlight for 2–4 weeks before using.

It is best to consume these flower oils within 3 months. If you want them to last longer, remove the flowers from the oil; they will then keep for 6 months or more.

Flowers for using with a light oil like sunflower:

rose petals or buds, lavender, English cowslip or jasmine.

Flowers for using with olive, hazelnut or walnut oil:

flowering herbs such as fennel, dill, basil, thyme, mint, marjoram, winter savoury and parsley.

FLOWER PETAL BUTTERS

Delicate sandwiches made with petal butters are perfect eaten in the garden on a summer's day. With the scent of flowers around you, imagine how delicious it is actually to be tasting in your mouth all those subtle aromas! Spread thinly cut bread with delicate flower butters; cut off the crusts to make tiny triangular sandwiches which you can eat in the garden under the shade of a sun umbrella or a leafy tree – or even stretched languorously in a hammock. Serve the sandwiches with a *tisane* (flower tea, see pages 136–137), or perhaps a cold, refreshing flowery drink like Pimms with borage, home-made lemonade with lemon balm or a chilled wine cup with rose petals (see pages 134–135).

To make flower butters

You can either impregnate the butter with the scents of the flowers by putting a layer of flowers in a glass dish and covering it with about 4oz/ 100g of unsalted butter (½ cup sweet butter), sliced in two. Press the butter onto the flowers, then press more flowers around the sides and over the top of the butter. Cover with cling film or foil and leave for about a day before using. If you are short of time, you can chop up lots of fresh, scented petals and mix them with butter and use immediately.

Good flowers to use are:

nasturtiums, honeysuckle, highly scented rose petals, jasmine, sweet geraniums, pot marigolds, lavender, clove carnations, primroses, English cowslips, violets and red clover.

right: Teatime on a summer's day amid the warm scents of the garden. A delicate sponge cake is scented with lilac – for decoration only – and daisies (Bellis perennis) (see page 130), accompanied by dainty flower-petal butter sandwiches (see above) and home-made cookies decorated with crystallized summer flowers (see page 132). A tisane is taken with this flowery tea – chamomile, passion flower or jasmine perhaps (see pages 136–137).

overleaf: The simplicity of a dish of baked trout with fennel and fennel flowers eaten, perhaps, by a lake full of lilies, will be appreciated by even the most discerning gourmet (see page 78). The variety of pelargoniums around the dish add colour but are not edible.

FLOWER PETAL JAMS

In mid-winter, when the evenings draw in, and teatime is often a meal eaten with the lights on because it is already dark outside, recall the glorious, hot summer days when all the flowers were in bloom by eating flower petal jams spread on wholemeal bread and butter or hot toast. These lovely jams not only look enticing, with flower petals suspended in clouds of pink and orange jam, but taste excellent, too. They can also be used to sandwich cakes together or to spread on biscuits, as flavourings in puddings and spooned over ice cream.

Useful tips on jam making

1. Always boil jam fast to get a good set, but make sure that the sugar is completely dissolved before boiling, or it may recrystallize in the jar.
2. During the boiling process, the jam will increase in volume, so always make it in a large preserving pan rather than a saucepan, which may not be big enough.
3. To test for set spoon a few drops of the jam on to a very cold plate. Leave for a few moments, then push the jam with your finger. If a wrinkled skin appears on the surface, the jam has reached setting point. If the surface does not wrinkle, continue to boil the jam for a further 5 minutes and test again.

previous page: The mystery and richness of the East are displayed in stunning colours with poppies and peonies, silks and brocades setting off Chinese stir-fried prawns and noodles with torn red carnation petals and bamboo shoots decorated with peony petals (see page 100). White chrysanthemums float in a finger bowl adding their own elegant touch to this exotic setting.

left: Christmas is a time of warmth, merriment and good food. Rosé punch with rose petals waits enticingly on the mantelpiece (see page 135). Stuffed flower turkey sits richly on the garlanded table accompanied by cranberry jelly with pinks, roast potatoes and julienne of carrots and courgettes (zucchini), which you can garnish with dried marjoram flowers if you have them (see pages 84–85). A Christmas cake lavishly decorated with crystallized flowers is stuffed with dried rose petals and violets (see page 10). Chocolates with crystallized petals wait temptingly for after the Christmas pudding.

ROSE PETAL JAM

This has been a traditional favourite for hundreds of years. You can find numerous recipes for this jam in all kinds of old cookery books.

2lb/900g highly scented rose petals
1lb/450g (2 cups) sugar
juice 1/2 lemon
fresh rose petals, to finish

Bring a pan of water to the boil, turn off the heat and put in 1lb/450g rose petals. Leave to steep for about 2 hours, then strain.

Measure 1pt/575ml (2½ cups) strained liquid into a preserving pan and add 1lb/450g (2 cups) sugar. Set over low heat and stir until the sugar has dissolved completely. Add a good squeeze of lemon juice and the remaining rose petals. Bring to the boil and boil until the jam reaches setting point. Remove from the heat and add some fresh rose petals. Mix well and leave to settle for 5 minutes before bottling the jam. Pour into hot jars and seal.

CRAB APPLE AND MALLOW JELLY

4lb/1.8kg crab apples
8 tablespoons mallow flower petals
sugar

Wash the crab apples and then chop them roughly, removing any stalks. Put them into a wide preserving pan with the mallow flowers and enough water to cover. Cook over low heat until soft. Stir the apples occasionally in case they stick to the bottom of the pan. Put the contents of the pan into a jelly bag and let it strain overnight.

Measure the juice and for each 1pt/575ml (2½ cups) add 1lb/450g (2 cups) sugar. Put the juice and sugar into a preserving pan and stir well over a low heat until all the sugar has dissolved. Turn up the heat and boil rapidly until setting point is reached. Pour the jelly into hot, clean jars and seal. You can add a few fresh mallow flowers at this point, if you wish. Stir them into the hot jelly pushing them well down so that they do not stay on the surface.

ELDERFLOWER JAM WITH GOOSEBERRIES

This jam has a really lovely flavour and will keep well. It is nice to eat it in mid-winter when the wind is howling outside and you can taste the summer fruit and remember the warmth and sunshine.

1lb/450g gooseberries, topped and tailed
4 heads elderflowers
1lb/450g (2 cups) sugar
juice 1 lemon
fresh elderflowers, to finish, optional

Combine all the ingredients in a preserving pan and slowly bring to the boil, stirring until all the sugar has dissolved. Boil rapidly for about 10 minutes, or until setting point is reached. Remove from the heat and leave for 5 minutes to allow the fruit and flowers to settle. If you prefer, you can remove the cooked flower heads at this point, or you can add a few fresh elderflowers and stir them well into the jam. Pour into hot jars and seal well.

APPLE AND MINT FLOWER JAM

This fragrant jam is good to eat at breakfast in the summer or for tea in winter on hot buttered toast.

3lb/1.4kg cooking apples
1/2pt/275ml (1¼ cups) water
2 tablespoons mint leaves
2lb/900g (4 cups) sugar
3 tablespoons mint flowers

Peel and core the apples and place them in a preserving pan with the water and mint leaves. Simmer gently until the apples are soft but not mushy. Stir in the sugar and mint flowers. Make sure that the sugar has completely dissolved, then increase the heat and bring the mixture to the boil. Boil rapidly until setting point has been reached. Leave in the pan for 5 minutes before pouring into hot, clean jars and sealing.

MAIN COURSES

'Food must pass through the eyes before it goes into the mouth.' This lovely and very apt old Mexican saying precisely emphasises what this book is all about – the effect that the visual impact of flowers has on our tastebuds, when presented with food. It is this excitement and delight at the visual presentation that can be exploited beautifully in the way main dishes are served in a meal.

Meat and fish can be magically transformed both visually and in flavour when cooked and garnished with a variety of glorious garden flowers. Who would have thought that a dish of quails cooked in wine with oranges could be so much enhanced by the addition of lavender (page 93)? The chicken in the Moroccan dish (page 95) is greatly changed and exceptionally flavoured by the liberal addition of rose petals. The marigold, an ancient pot herb, always gives a lift to stews and casseroles, while the richness of a pork dish can be offset by spicy herb flowers like marjoram and cooling ones like mint.

Fish is uplifted by the scents of spring flowers like English cowslips and primroses, while dill and fennel flowers give it a subtle spiciness. White meats go particularly well with flowers and the very delicate scent of lavender is perfect in Steamed Lavender Rabbit (page 91). Although it is unusual to use flowers with meat and fish, once you begin to do so you will find that all kinds of unexpected combinations go well together. So really let your imagination rip and enjoy being wildly imaginative in this challenging field!

FISH

SPRING FILLETS OF PLAICE WITH COWSLIPS OR CHIVE FLOWERS, LETTUCE HEARTS AND CHIVES

Serves 4

Accompany this dish with tiny new potatoes and a green vegetable.

8 plaice fillets, skinned
sea salt and black pepper
2–3 tablespoons chopped chives
8 teaspoons fresh English cowslips or chive flowers
1–2 lettuce hearts, finely chopped
3 tablespoons sunflower margarine
2 tablespoons flour
8 fl oz/225ml (1 cup) dry white wine
1 teaspoon grated lemon zest
whole fresh chives and flowers, to decorate

Heat the oven to 350F/180C/gas 4.

Season one side of each plaice fillet with salt and pepper, then place on each one some chopped chives, a teaspoon of English cowslips or chive flowers and some chopped lettuce heart. Roll up the fillets and secure with wooden cocktail sticks if necessary.

Grease a shallow ovenproof dish with a little of the margarine and arrange the stuffed fillets in the dish. Season lightly once more.

In a saucepan, melt the remaining margarine, stir in the flour and cook for 1 minute. Pour in the wine, stirring continuously, and cook gently until thickened. Add lemon zest to taste and pour the sauce over the plaice fillets. Cover the dish with foil and bake in the oven for 20–25 minutes.

Remove the foil and make a lattice pattern over the plaice fillets with the whole chives. Dot English cowslips or chive flowers in between the lattice and serve immediately while hot.

FISH AND FLOWER TERRINE

Serves 6

Serve the terrine with a crisp salad for a light summer lunch.

1lb/450g fresh leaf spinach or sorrel
8oz/225g white fish
1 sachet powdered gelatine
2 eggs, lightly beaten
5fl oz/150ml double cream (⅝ cup heavy cream)
freshly grated nutmeg
sea salt and black pepper
1 tablespoon chopped fresh dill or mixed fresh herbs (eg: tarragon, parsley and chervil)
3–4 tablespoons mixed summer flowers (eg: pansies, anchusa, chive flowers, nasturtiums, mallow)
8oz/225g crabmeat or shelled prawns (shrimps), chopped
butter for greasing
fresh flowers and herbs, to decorate

Blanch the spinach in boiling water, refresh in cold water, drain and dry on paper towels. Remove any stringy stalks. If you are using sorrel, do not blanch it.

Chop the white fish, discarding any skin and bones. Soak the gelatine in 3 tablespoons warm water. Mix together the chopped fish, soaked gelatine, eggs and cream and season with nutmeg, salt and pepper. Add your chosen chopped herbs, chop a few of the flowers and add these to the mixture. Reserve 4–6 tablespoons of the mixture.

In a separate bowl, lightly break up the crabmeat with a fork, or put in the chopped prawns (shrimps), and season lightly. Stir in the reserved fish mixture.

Heat the oven to 325F/160C/gas 3.

Grease a 1lb/450g terrine and line it with the spinach or sorrel leaves, bringing the leaves right up the sides and leaving an overhang at the top to fold over the final layer of fish.

Put in half the white fish mixture and cover it with a thick layer of flowers and a thin layer of spinach or sorrel. Spread over the crab or prawn (shrimp) mixture and cover with a thick layer of flowers and a thin layer of spinach or sorrel. Finally, spread over the rest of the white fish mixture and fold over the overhanging spinach or sorrel to cover the top completely.

Cover the terrine with a sheet of buttered greaseproof paper and place the dish in a roasting pan filled to a depth of 2in/5cm with boiling water. Bake in the oven for 45–50 minutes, until firm.

Leave the terrine to cool, then chill in the fridge. To serve, carefully turn out the terrine onto a pretty, flat plate and cut into thick slices. Decorate with fresh flowers and herbs.

FRUIT-STUFFED SOLE WITH ORANGES, GRAPES AND LILIES

Serves 4

Serve this unusual dish with tiny broad beans and duchesse potatoes.

4 fillets of sole
juice 2 limes
4oz/100g white grapes, peeled and seeded
1 orange, segmented, all white pith removed
6–8 lilies, shredded
butter, for greasing
8fl oz/225ml (1 cup) fish stock
4fl oz/125ml (½ cup) white wine
salt and pepper

Heat the oven to 350F/180C/gas 4.

Lay the sole fillets out flat, sprinkle with lime juice and leave to marinate for about 15 minutes. Skin the fillets, then stuff them with a mixture of grapes, orange segments and lilies. Season and roll up the fillets, securing them with wooden cocktail sticks.

Butter a shallow ovenproof dish and arrange the stuffed fillets in it. Sprinkle over a little lime juice and pour over the fish stock and wine. Cover tightly and cook in the oven for about 20 minutes.

Drain off the cooking liquid and keep the fillets warm. Strain the liquid into a pan and boil rapidly until reduced. Adjust the seasoning, pour the sauce over the sole fillets and serve.

BAKED TROUT WITH FENNEL AND FENNEL FLOWERS

Serves 2

Eat these delicious trout with summer vegetables or a salad – or just on their own with hot bread. Serve them on a bed of sliced, steamed Florence fennel with wedges of lemon.

2 tablespoons butter
2 fennel bulbs, sliced
2 tablespoons fennel flowers
2 large trout, cleaned
2 sprigs flowering fennel
salt and pepper
4fl oz/125ml (½ cup) white wine, or 2 tablespoons lemon juice

Heat the oven to 350F/180C/gas 4.

Use half the butter to grease a shallow ovenproof dish. Put in a layer of sliced fennel and fennel flowers and arrange the trout on top. Place a sprig of flowering fennel in each fish and season to taste. Pour over the wine or lemon juice, season and dot with butter.

Cover the dish with buttered foil and bake in the oven for about 15 minutes, until just cooked. Serve immediately.

PRAWNS (SHRIMP) IN HOT CHEESE SAUCE WITH VIOLETS AND CHIVES

Serves 4

This dish is best served on thick rounds of wholemeal toast with a side salad of cress, French parsley and cos lettuce.

1 tablespoon violets
1 tablespoon chopped chives
½pt/275ml (1¼ cups) milk
2 tablespoons butter
2 tablespoons flour
4oz/100g (1 cup) Gruyère cheese, grated
salt and pepper
1lb/450g prawns (shrimp), shelled

Place the violets and chives in the milk and heat to just below boiling point. Remove from the heat and leave to steep for about 15 minutes before making the sauce.

To make the sauce, melt the butter and stir in the flour. Cook for 1 minute, stirring. Gradually stir in the violet- and chive-flavoured milk and cook, beating well, to make a smooth sauce. Stir in the cheese and cook gently until it has melted completely. Season to taste, then stir in the prawns (shrimp) and heat through. Add a few fresh violets just before serving.

MUSSELS WITH SAFFRON

Serves 4

This is another of Alice B. Toklas's delightful recipes from *Aromas and Flavours of Past and Present*, which I have adapted.

4pt/2L (2 quarts) mussels
3 shallots, finely chopped
5 tablespoons butter
½ teaspoon saffron strands
3 egg yolks
1 tablespoon flour
8fl oz/225ml double cream (1 cup heavy cream)
2–3 tablespoons chopped parsley, to serve

Wash and scrub the mussels under cold running water and pull or cut away the beards. Discard any which are open or have broken shells.

Put the mussels in a saucepan with the shallots and butter, cover and cook over low heat, shaking the pan from time to time, until the steam escapes. Strain and reserve the juices and remove the mussels from their shells discarding any which are still closed.

Put the saffron strands in a pan and pour over the strained mussel juice. Mix together the egg yolks and flour and stir this mixture into the saffron-flavoured juice. Set the pan over low heat and cook, stirring continuously, until the sauce is thick enough to coat the back of a wooden spoon. Stir in the cream, heat through and pour the sauce over the mussels. Scatter over plenty of chopped parsley and serve at once.

SCENTED FISH-STUFFED VINE LEAVES

Serves 6

This deliciously spicy, scented dish goes well with brown or wild rice and crunchy, garden-fresh carrots. Serve the vine leaves on your best and most beautiful green and white dish.

1 tablespoon butter or oil
1 small onion, chopped
2 tomatoes, skinned and chopped
pinch grated nutmeg
pinch ground mace
3 tablespoons highly scented white rose petals
2 tablespoons fresh wholemeal breadcrumbs
2oz/50g (¼ cup) cooked white fish, flaked
1 egg, beaten
12 fresh or canned vine leaves
½ pint/275ml (1 cup) vegetable stock
5fl oz/150ml (⅝ cup) dry white wine
white rose petals, to garnish

Heat the oven to 350F/180C/gas 5.

Heat the butter or oil in a shallow pan, add the chopped onion and cook gently for 3 or 4 minutes, until the onion softens. Add the tomatoes, nutmeg and mace and cook for 1–2 minutes. Stir in 2 tablespoons of scented rose petals and the breadcrumbs and stir well.

Take the pan off the heat and stir in the fish and enough beaten egg to bind the mixture. Transfer the mixture to a bowl.

Blanch the vine leaves in boiling water for 1 minute. If you are using canned vine leaves, rinse off the brine. Lay the leaves out flat and place a spoonful of stuffing mixture in the centre of each. Add a few more rose petals to each one. Roll up the leaves, tucking in the ends, and secure with a wooden cocktail stick.

Arrange the stuffed vine leaves in a shallow ovenproof dish and pour over the vegetable stock and wine to cover. Cover the dish and cook in the oven for 30 minutes, or until the vine leaves are tender.

Serve immediately, garnished with fresh white rose petals.

SALMON BAKED IN A FOIL PARCEL WITH SPRING OR SUMMER FLOWERS

Serves 12–16

Serve the salmon with melted butter, black pepper and some fresh flowers; it is unbelievably delicious. If you are cooking the salmon in spring, use Parma violets, English cowslips or chive flowers. If you wait until summer, when wild salmon is cheaper, use squash flowers, pinks and red clover blossoms.

2oz/50g (¼ cup) butter, softened
1 x 5–6lb/2.3–2.7kg fresh salmon, cleaned
flowers in season (see note above)
4fl oz/125ml (½ cup) well-flavoured fish stock
2fl oz/50ml (¼ cup) dry white wine
melted butter, black pepper and fresh flowers, to serve

Heat the oven to 300F/150C/gas 2.

Spread most of the butter over the salmon and lay your chosen flowers on top. Place the salmon on a large piece of buttered foil and pour over the fish stock and wine. Fold the foil over the salmon and seal the edges to make a parcel. Place on a baking sheet and bake in the oven, allowing 12 minutes per lb/450g.

Carefully unwrap the salmon and serve on an oval dish, garnished with seasonal flowers.

SCALLOPS IN WINE SAUCE WITH MUSTARD FLOWERS

Serves 4

Mustard flowers are readily available in the English countryside and add a delightful touch to seafood.

½pt/275ml (1¼ cups) milk
1–2 tablespoons mustard flowers
8 scallops, cleaned and shells reserved
4fl oz/125ml (½ cup) fish stock
4fl oz/125ml (½ cup) white wine
1 tablespoon butter
2 tablespoons flour
freshly grated nutmeg
sea salt and white pepper
mustard flowers and hot toast, to serve

Heat the milk and mustard flowers until warm and leave to steep.

Remove the scallops from their shells and keep the shells warm. Briefly poach the scallops in the fish stock and wine; do not cook them for more than 3 or 4 minutes or they will become rubbery and tasteless. Remove from the poaching liquid and set aside. Strain and reserve the liquid.

Melt the butter in a pan, stir in the flour and cook for 1 minute. Strain in the milk in which the mustard flowers were steeped and stir well. Add some of the poaching liquid from the scallops and cook gently, stirring continuously, to make a creamy sauce. Season with a little nutmeg, salt and pepper.

Replace the scallops in their warmed shells, pour over the sauce and decorate with fresh mustard flowers. Serve immediately with fingers of hot toast.

POULTRY, GAME AND MEAT

FLOWER DUCK

Serves 4

This tasty and dramatic Chinese dish is quoted by Florence White in her book *Flowers as Food*. The Chinese use a lot of flowers in their cuisine and are especially fond of Tiger lilies. I have adapted this recipe for practical reasons and have also suggested an alternative method of cooking the duck.

If Tiger lilies are not available, use Enchantment lilies instead. Serve the duck with wild or fried rice and some crunchy green vegetables.

1 × 4lb/1.8kg duck
1 bay leaf
½ teaspoon allspice berries, crushed
Tiger lilies
1 teaspoon cornflour (cornstarch)
1 teaspoon soy sauce

Place the duck in a heavy pan and pour over just enough water to cover. Add the bay leaf and crushed allspice, cover the pan tightly and cook slowly for 2½–3 hours, until the duck is tender. After 30 minutes, add 4 or 5 Tiger lilies, which will give a subtle, aromatic flavour to the duck.

When the duck is cooked, slice it thinly. Keep warm.

Strain the duck stock, return it to the pan and boil until slightly reduced. Make a paste from the cornflour (cornstarch) and soy sauce and stir into the stock. Boil for 1 minute, until thickened. Pour the sauce over the sliced duck, decorate with lots of Tiger lilies and serve.

Alternative Recipe

Stuff the duck with a mixture of cooked wild rice, chopped Tiger lilies, lightly fried spring onions (scallions), slivers of garlic, a few crushed allspice berries and seasoning. Sprinkle soy sauce over the duck and roast it at 350F/180C/gas 4, allowing 20 minutes per lb/450g.

When the duck is cooked and deliciously brown and aromatic, serve it with a dash of soy sauce, surrounded by Tiger lilies.

SPICY STUFFED FLOWER TURKEY

It is a pity that we tend only to serve a turkey at festivals like Christmas, Easter and Thanksgiving; it is such an excellent bird which deserves to be eaten more often. It is very economical, since it has virtually no fat and it tastes just as good served hot or cold.

This recipe is suitable for any occasion. The turkey is stuffed with a spicy, flowery mixture and cooked until brown and crackly on the outside, but very juicy on the inside. Eat it hot or cold, with or without a sauce and the usual accompaniments and serve it with lots of exciting vegetables: minty courgettes (zucchini), julienne of carrots with marjoram flowers and puréed celeriac with grapes and oranges – and flower-flavoured cranberry jelly.

Serves 8–10

Stock

turkey giblets (not the liver)
1 carrot
1 onion
sprig parsley
salt and pepper

1 x 10lb/4.6kg turkey

Stuffing

2oz/50g (¼ cup) butter
2 onions, finely chopped
2 dessert apples, peeled, cored and chopped
6oz/175g (1½ cups) fresh brown and white breadcrumbs, mixed
1 tablespoon fresh or dried marjoram leaves
1 tablespoon fresh or dried marjoram flowers
10 fresh or dried nasturtium leaves, chopped
4 tablespoons fresh or dried nasturtium flowers
2 tablespoons sultanas

fresh or dried flower petals or nasturtiums, to garnish

First, make the stock. Put the giblets in a pan with the carrot, onion and parsley. Cover with water, season and bring to the boil. Cover the pan and simmer gently for about 1 hour, to make a good rich stock. Set aside.

Heat the oven to 325F/160C/gas 3.

Heat 1 tablespoon butter in a frying pan, put in the chopped onions and sauté over medium heat for about 2 minutes, until soft but not brown. Add the chopped apple and cook for a further 1–2 minutes. Stir in the breadcrumbs, marjoram leaves and flowers, nasturtium leaves and flowers and the sultanas. Stir well to coat the mixture with butter, adding a little more butter if necessary. Season to taste and stuff the turkey with this mixture. Weigh the stuffed turkey.

Rub the turkey all over with butter, season and cover with buttered foil. Pour in the prepared stock to a depth of about 1in/2cm, then put in the turkey. Roast in the oven, allowing 20 minutes per lb/450g. Turn the turkey over several times during cooking, so that it has periods of cooking breast-down; this will keep it very succulent and the breast and legs will cook evenly. Add more stock to the pan as necessary.

Serve the turkey on a large oval platter, surrounded by roast potatoes and garnished with dried or fresh petals or nasturtiums. Make a rich gravy from the pan juices and hand it round separately, in a sauceboat.

CHICKEN IN A MELON WITH HONEYSUCKLE

Serves 4

This makes a stunning-looking dish for a summer buffet table and would be equally good as a starter for a dinner party.

4 Ogen, Charentais or Galia melons
8oz/225g (2 cups) cooked chicken, diced
4oz/100g (1 cup) white grapes, peeled and seeded
3 tablespoons honeysuckle flowers
5fl oz/150ml (⅝ cup) home-made mayonnaise (see page 62)
honeysuckle sprigs, to garnish

Halve the melons and discard the seeds. Scoop out the flesh with a melon baller and set aside. Turn the empty melon halves upside down and leave to drain.

Mix together the diced chicken, grapes and honeysuckle with the mayonnaise and pile the mixture into the drained melon shells. Chill well and served topped with a sprig of honeysuckle.

MARINATED PORK CHOPS WITH MINT LEAVES AND FLOWERS

Serves 4

The minty taste of this dish offsets the richness of the pork and makes it refreshing and different.

4 fl oz/125 ml (½ cup) sunflower oil
juice 2 limes or lemons
freshly milled black pepper
3 tablespoons mint leaves and flowers
4 pork chops
mint flowers, to garnish

Mix together the oil, lime or lemon juice, pepper and mint flowers and leaves. Pour over the chops and leave to marinate for 1–2 hours.

Heat the grill to high.

Drain the chops and grill for about 15 minutes, turning once and basting occasionally with the marinade.

Garnish with mint flowers and serve with buttered and minted new potatoes and crisp French beans.

right: Wonderful, spicy Eastern flavours suffuse this glorious Moroccan dish which is made with cinnamon-fried chicken, dried apricots, pine kernels and pistachios, pot marigolds, rose petals and rose water (see page 95).

overleaf: Barbecued fish kebabs with thyme and mint flowers can be dressed up for a special summer feast (see page 97). Flowers from the garden set off the rich colours of peppers and bay leaves which are cooked with the fish.

STEAMED LAVENDER CHICKEN OR RABBIT

Serves 4

Crunchy broccoli and wild rice go well with this aromatic dish.

sprigs flowering lavender
4 chicken or rabbit portions
2 tablespoons butter
1 tablespoon flour
salt and pepper

Put a few sprigs of flowering lavender in the bottom of a steamer and place the chicken or rabbit portions in the top. Steam for 20–30 minutes, until the meat is just tender; it should still be nice and juicy. Keep warm.

Melt the butter in a saucepan, stir in the flour and cook, stirring, for 2 minutes. Pour in enough of the lavender-flavoured water from the steamer to give a sauce of the consistency you like, bring to the boil and simmer for 5 minutes. Season to taste.

Slice the meat and serve, covered in pale lavender sauce. Decorate each portion with a sprig of flowering lavender.

previous page: A stylish, elegant and spicy dish from the Orient: Chinese flower duck roasted in soy sauce and stuffed with spicy day or tiger lilies (see page 83). A dish fit for an emperor.

left: The smell of the sea wafts through this cold seafood pasta dish with its sparkling fresh crustaceans, squid, green tagliatelle and brilliant chive flowers (see page 102). The bowl crammed with flowers for decoration adds a colourful touch.

FRAGRANT CASSEROLE OF ROSE DUCK

Serves 4

The addition of fragrant rose petals to this casserole gives it a rather special distinction; use the most fragrant petals available. Attractive presentation is particularly important in this dish – serve the duck on a shallow platter and arrange the chestnuts, orange segments and rose petals like a beautiful picture to stimulate the taste buds of your guests. Serve the duck with lots of green vegetables and creamed potatoes and choose a lightly chilled rosé wine with a few rose petals floating on it.

2oz/50g (¼ cup) butter
4 duck portions (leg or breast)
12 baby onions
16 chestnuts, peeled
3 tablespoons highly scented rose petals (red are best)
1 orange, segmented
1–2 tablespoons flour
4fl oz/125ml (½ cup) chicken stock
4fl oz/125ml (½ cup) red wine
salt and pepper
orange segments and rose petals, to garnish

Heat the oven to 325F/170C/gas 3.

Heat the butter in a frying pan until foaming. Put in the duck and fry until browned on all sides. Using a slotted spoon, transfer the duck pieces to a casserole.

Put the whole onions in the pan and fry until brown. Add the chestnuts and cook for 2–3 minutes. With a slotted spoon, transfer the onions and chestnuts to the casserole with the duck. Toss in the rose petals and add the orange segments.

Add enough flour to the frying pan to absorb all the butter and cook for 2 minutes, stirring. Add the stock and wine, bring to the boil and season to taste. Pour the sauce over the duck. Cover the casserole and cook in the oven for about 1 hour, until the duck is tender.

Arrange the duck pieces on an oval platter and surround them with the onions and chestnuts. Garnish with orange segments and fresh rose petals and serve with sauce separately in a sauceboat.

BRAISED QUAILS WITH THYME, LAVENDER AND ORANGES

Serves 4

The quails take on the heady scent of the lavender and thyme, which is nicely offset by the flavour of oranges. Serve the plump, juicy quails with creamed potatoes and tiny Brussels sprouts.

2 tablespoons butter
4 quails
8 shallots, halved
1–2 tablespoons flour
8 fl oz/225ml (1 cup) red wine
8 fl oz/225ml (1 cup) chicken stock
sea salt and black pepper
4 sprigs thyme and thyme flowers
1½ tablespoons lavender flowers
grated zest and juice 1 orange
1 teaspoon cornflour (cornstarch), optional
fresh orange segments and fresh lavender flowers, to garnish

Heat the oven to 325F/170C/gas 3.

In a heavy pan, heat the butter until foaming. Put in the quails and brown them all over. Using a slotted spoon, transfer the quails to a casserole large enough to take all the birds in one layer.

Add the shallots to the frying pan and sauté for 2 minutes. With a slotted spoon, transfer them to the casserole. Add to the frying pan enough flour to absorb all the butter and cook, stirring, for 2 minutes. Pour in enough wine and stock to give a thin sauce, bring to the boil, then season to taste. Stir in the thyme and lavender and the orange zest and juice, pour over the quails. Cover the casserole and cook in the oven for 30–40 minutes, until the quails are tender.

Transfer the quails to the serving dish. If you wish, thicken the sauce by boiling hard for a few minutes, or thicken it with 1 teaspoon cornflour (cornstarch). Pour the sauce over the quails and serve garnished with fresh orange segments and lavender flowers.

SWEET LAMB CASSEROLE WITH PEARL BARLEY AND MARIGOLDS

Serves 4

This casserole has a very pleasing, distinctive flavour.

2 tablespoons sunflower oil
2 onions, finely chopped
2 carrots, finely sliced
1lb/450g lean lamb fillet, diced
2 tablespoons pearl barley
10–15fl oz/275–425ml (1¼–2 cups) hot beef or chicken stock
3 tablespoons marigold petals*
salt and pepper
1–2 tablespoons butter, optional
1–2 tablespoons flour, optional

Heat the oven to 325F/170C/gas 3.

Heat the oil in a large pan. Put in the onions and carrots and fry for 2–3 minutes. Using a slotted spoon, transfer them to a casserole.

Quickly fry the lamb in the oil, turning until browned all over, then add the lamb to the casserole.

Put the barley in the casserole and pour over enough hot stock to cover the contents. Add the marigold petals and season to taste.

Cook in the oven for 1½–2 hours, until the barley and lamb are cooked. If you like a thick gravy, mix together the butter and flour, add them to the gravy and bring to the boil. Simmer for 3 minutes, until thickened.

Just before serving, add a few fresh marigold petals.

*Make certain that you use a pot marigold (*Calendula*) rather than an African marigold (*Tagetes*).

MOROCCAN CHICKEN WITH PISTACHIOS, APRICOTS, ROSES AND MARIGOLDS

Serves 6–8

I serve this spicy dish in a large, wide Moroccan bowl; it looks, smells and tastes wonderful. It is covered in rose petals and the aroma of the flowers and cinnamon is quite fantastic.

1lb/450g (2 cups) long grain rice
2 tablespoons vegetable oil
3 spring onions (scallions)
1 onion, finely chopped
2oz/50g plump dried apricots, chopped
2oz/50g pistachio nuts, shelled
2oz/50g pine kernels
1–2 tablespoons ground cinnamon
1 × 3lb/1.4kg chicken, skinned, boned and cut into strips
sea salt and black pepper
1 teaspoon rose water
1 heaped tablespoon highly scented rose petals
1 heaped teaspoon marigold petals*

Cook the rice in boiling, salted water for 15–20 minutes, or until just tender; it should still be a little chewy.

Heat 1 tablespoon oil in a frying pan, put in the onions and fry quickly for 2 minutes. Add the apricots, pistachios and pine kernels, sprinkling them with cinnamon as they cook. Using a slotted spoon, remove the mixture from the pan and stir into the rice. Cover and keep warm.

Heat the remaining oil, put in the chicken strips and fry quickly, sprinkling with a little more cinnamon. Do not overcook the chicken, which should be tender and juicy. Mix the cooked chicken into the rice, season if necessary and spread the mixture in a wide shallow dish. Sprinkle with rose water and decorate with the rose and marigold petals.

Serve at once.

STIR-FRY AND BARBECUES

STIR-FRIED FRESH CRAB WITH GINGER AND YELLOW AND RED NASTURTIUMS

Serves 4

white and brown meat from 1 fresh crab
1–2 tablespoons sunflower oil
8 spring onions (scallions), sliced
2in/5cm piece fresh ginger root, grated
3 garlic cloves, crushed
1 tablespoon chopped chives
few drops of light soy sauce
3 tablespoons mixed yellow and red nasturtium flowers
Chinese noodles or rice, to serve
fresh nasturtium flowers, to garnish

Heat the oil in a wok until smoking. Toss in the onions, stir and add the grated ginger, garlic and chives. Reduce the heat slightly and stir-fry for a few seconds. Put in the crabmeat and stir-fry for no more than 1 minute, until hot. Add soy sauce to taste and the nasturtium flowers.

Serve on a bed of Chinese noodles or rice and decorate with a flower or two.

LEMON-GRILLED BARBECUED HERRING WITH LEMON THYME AND ROSEMARY

Serves 4

4 tablespoons lemon thyme
2–3 tablespoons rosemary flowers
4 fresh herrings, cleaned
2 tablespoons vegetable oil
4 whole sprigs lemon thyme
salt and pepper
chunks of wholemeal bread and butter, lemon wedges, to serve

Heat a charcoal barbecue until smouldering.

Press the lemon thyme and rosemary flowers onto both sides of the herrings, brush with oil and place a sprig of lemon thyme inside each fish. Season with salt and pepper and grill on the barbecue, brushing with oil and turning occasionally. Decorate with thyme and rosemary flowers before serving.

BARBECUED FISH KEBABS WITH THYME AND MINT FLOWERS

Serves 6–8

Serve these tasty kebabs with a crisp, colourful salad of endive, rocket, salad burnet, radicchio and lots of fresh herbs and flowers.

1½–2lb/700–900g monkfish
12–24 bay leaves
1 yellow pepper, seeded and cubed
1 red pepper, seeded and cubed
3–4 onions, quartered

Marinade

4fl oz/125ml (½ cup) olive oil
juice 1 lemon
1 teaspoon dry mustard
2 garlic cloves, crushed
2 tablespoons mixed thyme and mint flowers
salt and black pepper

Heat a charcoal barbecue until smouldering.

Cut the monkfish into 1-in/2.5cm cubes. Combine all the marinade ingredients, put in the monkfish and marinate for 1 hour.

Thread the kebabs onto wooden skewers in the following order: bay leaf, yellow pepper, fish cube, red pepper, onion quarter and so on until all the ingredients are used up.

Sprinkle the assembled kebabs with thyme and mint flowers, then cook them quickly on the glowing barbecue for about 5 minutes, turning once. Decorate with lots of fresh flowers before serving.

BARBECUED LAMB KEBABS WITH HONEY AND ROSEMARY

Serves 4

12oz–1lb/350–450g lamb fillet, cut into 1in/2.5cm cubes
8 large or 16 small field mushrooms
1 lemon, sliced thickly
1 orange, sliced thickly
4 tablespoons honey (rosemary honey, if possible)
2 teaspoons lavender flowers and leaves, mixed
flowering rosemary, to garnish

Thread the lamb cubes, mushrooms (halve them if they are large), lemon and orange slices onto 4 skewers. Pour 1 tablespoon honey over each and leave to marinate with the lavender flowers and leaves for about 1 hour, turning the skewers occasionally, so that the kebabs are coated with honey.

Heat the grill or a barbecue until hot.

Grill for 8–12 minutes, turning several times during cooking.

Decorate each kebab with a sprig of flowering rosemary and serve with a salad of cos lettuce dressed with walnut oil.

STIR-FRIED CHICKEN BREASTS WITH COURGETTE (ZUCCHINI) FLOWERS

Serves 4

Use individual Chinese bowls for this dish and serve it with a side dish of plain boiled rice.

1 tablespoon sunflower oil
8 spring onions (scallions), sliced diagonally
½ red pepper, seeded and cut into strips
2 garlic cloves, slivered
½lb/225g French beans, thinly sliced
black pepper
dark soy sauce
4 chicken breast fillets, cut into thin strips
8 courgette (zucchini) flowers

Heat the oil in a wok until smoking, put in the onions, red pepper, garlic and beans and stir fry for 3 minutes. Sprinkle with black pepper and soy sauce to taste. Add the chicken strips and cook for a further 3–4 minutes, until the chicken is just cooked, but still tender and juicy. Add the courgette (zucchini) flowers, fry for a few seconds, then transfer everything to a serving dish, or serve from the wok.

STIR-FRIED SWEET AND SOUR FISH WITH CHICKWEED AND MARIGOLDS

Serves 4

1–2 tablespoons sunflower oil
6–8 spring onions (scallions), sliced diagonally
2–3 garlic cloves, crushed
1in/2cm piece fresh ginger root, grated
1lb/450g fresh white fish (eg: sole, coley, cod or plaice)
3 tablespoons flowering chickweed
2 tablespoons marigold petals*

Sauce

1½ tablespoons cornflour (cornstarch)
2–3 tablespoons wine vinegar
1½ tablespoons tomato paste
1½ tablespoons soy sauce
3 tablespoons orange juice
2 tablespoons soft dark brown sugar

Chinese noodles or boiled rice, to serve

First make the sauce. Blend the cornflour (cornstarch) with vinegar to taste, then stir in the tomato paste and finally all the other ingredients.

Heat the oil in a wok over high heat until smoking. Add the onions, garlic and ginger and stir-fry for 1–2 minutes. Flake the fish or cut it into small pieces and add to the wok, together with half the flowers. Stir-fry for 1 minute, then pour in the sauce and cook for a further 2 minutes. Serve piping hot on a bed of Chinese noodles or rice and garnish with the remaining chickweed and pot marigold petals.

*Make certain that you use a pot marigold (*Calendula*) rather than an African marigold (*Tagetes*).

STIR-FRIED PRAWNS WITH CHRYSANTHEMUMS AND CARNATIONS

Serves 4

Float white chrysanthemums in small finger bowls for a pretty, decorative effect and serve a side dish of stir-fried bamboo shoots with a few peony petals, for decoration only.

8–12oz/225–350g Chinese egg noodles
1–2 tablespoons sunflower oil
6 spring onions (scallions), sliced diagonally
3 garlic cloves, slivered
1in/2cm piece fresh ginger root, peeled and grated
1lb/450g fresh prawns (shrimp), peeled
petals 1 large white chrysanthemum head
1–2 tablespoons light soy sauce
½ fresh lime
dark red petals 1 large red carnation

Cook the noodles in plenty of boiling, salted water for 3–4 minutes. Drain, heap into a large serving dish and keep warm.

Meanwhile, heat the oil in a round-bottomed wok until smoking. Toss in the onions, garlic and ginger and stir well for 1 minute. Add the prawns (shrimp) and chrysanthemum petals and stir-fry for a further 2 minutes. Add soy sauce to taste and a squeeze of lime juice, then a few shredded carnation petals.

Pour the prawn (shrimp) mixture over the noodles and decorate with the remaining petals. Serve at once, giving each guest an individual bowl and chopsticks to help themselves.

PETAL PASTAS

We are quite accustomed to combining pasta with a variety of meats and fish, eggs and cheese, so why not be bolder and use flower petals with pasta? You will find that the flavour and colours of the petals greatly enhance both the look and the taste of the dishes and it is also great fun to experiment with different flowers.

In the Rose and Poppy Seed pasta (page 106), the brilliance of the petals and the grainy dark seeds give the dish a really stylish appearance, quite apart from the delicious taste. The purple pansies dotted among the brightly coloured peppers make the Pepper pasta (pages 102–103) a feast for the eyes as well as the stomach! There are all kinds of flowers you could use and I have only given you a taste of what could be. So, make up your own petal pasta dishes from the great variety of edible flowers at your disposal. Remember that both colour and taste are important here. What you see excites the tastebuds and, in the end, makes the dish rewarding. Create your own beautiful pictures with pasta and petals and have fun!

COLD SEAFOOD PASTA

Serves 4

This refreshing pasta dish is equally delicious served hot, in which case, just heat the seafood in a little olive oil before serving.

8oz/225g green tagliatelle
2 tablespoons olive oil
1 teaspoon lemon juice
3 garlic cloves, crushed
sea salt and black pepper
1lb/450g prawns (shrimp)
2oz/50g prepared squid, cleaned and very thinly sliced
8oz/225g crab meat
chopped chives, chive flowers and coriander leaves, to garnish

Cook the tagliatelle in plenty of boiling, salted water until 'al dente'. Drain, toss with the oil, the lemon juice and garlic, season with sea salt and pepper and leave to cool.

Shell half the prawns (shrimp), reserving the remainder.

Arrange the tagliatelle on a large platter. Place the squid, shelled prawns (shrimp) and crab meat on the pasta and decorate with chives and coriander. Arrange the unshelled prawns (shrimp) around the edge of the platter and garnish with whole chive flowers.

PEPPER PASTA WITH PANSIES

Serves 4

The delight of this dish is the texture and colours. The chewy wholewheat spirals act as an excellent foil for the sweet, crunchy taste of the peppers, while the purple pansies lend the dish elegance and style. Serve this with a side dish of green vegetables in season.

8–10oz/225–275g wholewheat pasta spirals
2 tablespoons olive oil
1 red pepper, thinly sliced
1 yellow pepper, thinly sliced
3 spring onions (scallions), sliced diagonally
salt and pepper
1 heaped tablespoon purple pansy petals, to garnish

Cook the pasta spirals in plenty of boiling, salted water for about 10 minutes, until 'al dente'. Drain, toss in a little olive oil and keep warm.

Put the remaining oil into a heavy frying pan, together with the sliced peppers and onions. Fry quickly for 2–3 minutes. Drain and mix the vegetables with the pasta. Season to taste and scatter in the pansy petals just before serving.

MONKFISH PASTA WITH MARIGOLDS AND ANCHUSA

Serves 4

This deliciously fishy pasta is enhanced by the flavour and colour of the marigold and anchusa petals. The fresh herbs and cream add their own texture and flavour. Do use fresh pasta rather than dried for this dish; it will be far better. Serve with buttered spinach and a fresh tomato salad.

12oz/350g monkfish, cubed
½pt/275ml (1¼ cups) good fish stock
10–12oz/275–350g fresh white or green tagliatelle
1 tablespoon butter
1 tablespoon each chopped fresh coriander, dill, parsley and chives
salt and pepper
5fl oz/150ml single cream (⅝ cup light cream)
1 tablespoon marigold petals*
2 teaspoons anchusa flowers

Poach the monkfish in the fish stock for about 10 minutes, until just done. Drain and keep warm.

Cook the pasta in plenty of boiling, salted water for 3–4 minutes, until 'al dente'. Drain, toss in the butter and keep warm.

Mix together the herbs, fish and pasta and season to taste. Warm the cream in a heavy pan, then pour it over the pasta. Serve in a beautiful bowl, tossing in the flower petals at the last moment.

*Make certain that you use a pot marigold (*Calendula*) rather than an African marigold (*Tagetes*).

BUCKWHEAT NOODLES DECKED OUT IN RED AND BLUE

Serves 4

12oz/350g buckwheat noodles
2 tablespoons sunflower oil
1 onion, chopped
1 garlic clove, crushed
1lb/450g fresh tomatoes, skinned and chopped or 1 × 15oz/400g canned
tomatoes
1 tablespoon tomato paste
salt and pepper
1 tablespoon basil leaves, torn
1–2 tablespoons anchusa flowers

Cook the noodles in plenty of boiling, salted water until 'al dente'.
Drain, toss in a little oil and keep warm.

Heat the remaining oil. Add the onion and garlic and fry gently for 2–3
minutes, until soft. Add the tomatoes, bring to the boil, then simmer,
uncovered, until the sauce has reduced slightly. Stir in the tomato paste
and season to taste. Stir in the basil leaves and some of the anchusa
flowers, reserving a few for garnish. Pour the sauce over the noodles,
sprinkle with flowers and serve at once.

HOT BUTTERED TAGLIATELLE WITH BASIL AND DANDELIONS

Serves 4

12oz/350g fresh tagliatelle
1 tablespoon olive oil
1 teaspoon lemon juice
1 tablespoon fresh basil leaves, torn
2oz/50g (½ cup) pistachio nuts, shelled
1 teaspoon dandelion petals
sea salt and black pepper

Cook the tagliatelle in plenty of boiling, salted water until 'al dente'.
Drain and toss in the olive oil and lemon juice. Add the basil leaves,
pistachios and dandelion petals, season to taste and
serve at once.

BLUE CHEESE PASTA WITH BERGAMOT

Serves 4

You can use any kind of blue cheese for this dish – stilton, dolcelatte and
gorgonzola are all excellent with either wholewheat spaghetti or home-
made noodles. The brilliant red bergamot flowers add a wonderful
splash of colour and give the dish a spicy flavour.

Serve the pasta with a crunchy side salad for a really appetizing meal.

10–12oz/225–275g wholewheat spaghetti or home-made noodles
2 tablespoons fresh parsley, very finely chopped
2 tablespoons sesame or walnut oil
salt and pepper
6–8oz/175–225g blue cheese, crumbled
petals of 8 red bergamot flowers

Cook the pasta in plenty of boiling, salted water until 'al dente'. Drain
and transfer to a serving dish. Toss in the parsley and oil and season to
taste. Sprinkle on the cheese, then toss in the bergamot petals. Serve
immediatcly.

ROSE AND POPPY SEED PASTA

Serves 4

This spicy pasta is greatly enhanced by its exotic colours – the bright red rose petals and the deep purple poppy seeds. It is an easy dish to make and is light, yet surprisingly filling. Serve it for lunch on a warm summer's day with a crisp green salad.

10oz/275g pasta shells
2 tablespoons sunflower oil
1 onion, sliced into thin rings
2 garlic cloves, crushed
2 teaspoons poppy seeds
sea salt and black pepper
1 heaped tablespoon red rose petals

Cook the pasta shells in plenty of boiling, salted water until 'al dente'. Drain, toss in a little sunflower oil and keep warm.

Put the remaining oil in a pan with the onion rings and sweat gently until the onion is soft but not browned. Lift out the onion with a slotted spoon and mix in with the pasta shells.

Put the garlic into the oil in which the onions were cooked and fry, stirring, for 1 minute. Mix the cooked garlic into the pasta.

Toss the pasta in a warmed serving bowl or dish and sprinkle over the poppy seeds and seasoning to taste. Just before serving, throw in the rose petals.

right: Spring is here and with it comes the perfume of fresh violets, daffodils and hyacinths in abundance. Primavera salad with exotic fruits and violets (see page 112); butter cookies with crystallized violets (see page 132); crystallized daffodil – lovely as a decoration but not to be eaten – with fresh fruits, and spring rhubarb fool with grape hyacinths (see page 112).

overleaf: Cool, cool for summer – a cold delight set in marble folds – exotic lavender sorbet (see page 126) with scented-leaved geranium ice cream (see page 120) and rose petal sorbet (see page 125). The variety of pelargoniums around the base are used purely for decoration.

DESSERTS

In this section of the book everyone will feel at home, since flowers are natural ingredients to add to fruit, creams, tarts and jellies. Their superb colours will shine through every dessert and the flavours will be quite amazing.

Use flowers liberally in jellies, pancakes, fools and tarts. You can try different combinations instead of those I have suggested. Use tiny petals and buds in miniature patterns for spectacular garnishes and always decorate each dessert with the same kind of flowers you have used in cooking it.

Flower fritters (see page 115) are favourites with everyone. Dip the fresh flowers into the batter, fry quickly and eat immediately accompanied by slices of lemon and a little caster sugar. It is best to pick the flowers you want to use straight out of your garden, if you can. This will give the desserts the best possible flavour.

Choose all the most highly scented flowers for desserts, like honeysuckle, old-fashioned roses, violets, primroses, English cowslips, meadowsweet, passion flowers, jasmine, lavender, sweet woodruff and chamomile.

To make fruit salads special, add a few drops of rose or orange flower water as well as a dash of flower liqueur and garnish with fresh flowers.

When serving desserts remember that it is the visual picture which will most impress your guests.

previous page: Fresh desserts for a summer dinner party include fruit and flower jelly (see pages 114–115), mouth-watering raspberry snow scented with white stocks (see page 113) and crispy, fragrant elderflower fritters (see page 115).

left: Tulips are used in a decorative way to set the scene for delectable glâce de Jasmin (see page 122) and rose petal ice cream luxuriously piled in a flower ice bowl for a very special occasion (see page 119).

PRIMAVERA SALAD WITH VIOLETS AND EXOTIC FRUITS

In a beautiful glass bowl combine the following fruits: sliced mango, kiwi fruit, fresh lychees, apples, oranges and grapefruit, fresh pineapple, banana, paw paw (papaya) and melon. Add some twists of orange and lemon peel, a squeeze of fresh lemon juice, about a dozen violets and a sprig or two of lemon balm. Leave in a cool place for 1 hour.

If there is not enough juice from the fruit, add a little sugar syrup and a dash of your favourite liqueur, if you like.

Just before serving, add a few drops of rose water or orange flower water and some more fresh violets.

Serve slightly chilled with madeleines or home-made biscuits (cookies). You can also decorate them with crystallized flowers (violets would be appropriate) if you like.

SPRING RHUBARB WITH GRAPE HYACINTHS

Serves 4

1lb/450g young rhubarb
2–3 tablespoons raw brown sugar
juice and zest ½ orange
a few grape hyacinths, to garnish

Cut the rhubarb into 1in/2cm chunks. Place in a heavy pan with just enough sugar to sweeten without taking away the 'bite'. Add the orange juice and zest to taste and slowly bring to the boil. Reduce the heat, cover the pan and simmer gently for 5–7 minutes, until the rhubarb is soft. Purée in a blender or food processor until smooth. Pour into small bowls and serve sprinkled with a few florets of grape hyacinths, which give the rhubarb a wonderful scented taste. Serve with home-made shortbread.

FRESH RASPBERRY SNOW WITH SWEET WOODRUFF OR WHITE STOCKS

Serves 4–6

1lb/450g fresh raspberries
2 tablespoons caster sugar
½pt/275ml double cream (1¼ cups heavy cream), whipped
raspberries and raspberry leaves, to decorate
sprigs flowering sweet woodruff or white stocks, to garnish

Sieve the raspberries and stir in sugar to taste. Blend them into the whipped cream and pile into individual dessert dishes. Serve chilled, decorated with raspberries and leaves and sprigs of woodruff or white stocks.

LAVENDER JELLY

This exotic and gorgeously pretty jelly comes from John McGeever of Congham Hall in Norfolk and can be eaten both as a superb dessert with, perhaps, a little cream, or as an unusual accompaniment to roast game or rabbit.

7fl oz/200ml (⅞ cup) dry champagne or dry white wine
7fl oz/200ml (⅞ cup) unsweetened apple juice
2fl oz/50ml (¼ cup) crème de cassis
2oz/50g (¼ cup) sugar
2 tablespoons lemon juice
1oz/25g (⅛ cup) lavender flowers
4 teaspoons gelatine
4 tablespoons water

Gently heat the champagne or white wine with the apple juice, crème de cassis, sugar and lemon juice. Pour onto the lavender flowers and leave, covered, to infuse for about 10 minutes. Sprinkle the gelatine onto 4 tablespoons water and leave to soften, then heat gently until the gelatine is completely dissolved.

Strain the lavender liquid, pressing it to extract all the juices. Warm the lavender liquid and add the dissolved gelatine. Stir and strain again through a fine sieve or muslin. Leave to cool and set. The jelly will keep for about 14 days in a fridge.

LADIES BENEATH THE SHEETS

Serves 2

I invented this amusing dessert for a male chauvinist who liked to entertain young ladies in his apartment. I am ashamed to admit that I invented quite a number of 'seduction' recipes for this man! This one is just for fun and the appearance of the bumpy pears under their 'sheet' of cream decorated with tiny rose petals must have caused much laughter.

2 pears, peeled
8fl oz/225ml (1 cup) red wine
1 clove
1 small stick cinnamon
2–3 tablespoons vanilla sugar
5fl oz/150ml double cream (⁵/₈ cup heavy cream)
tiny rose petals, to decorate
sponge fingers, to serve

Poach the pears with the wine, clove, cinnamon and vanilla sugar to taste until they are tender. Leave to cool, then drain and cut in half. Lay the pears, flat side down, in a pretty dish. Just before serving, pour over the cream and scatter the rose petals over the top, in a pattern if you like. Serve with sponge fingers and a smile on your face!

SUMMER FRUIT AND FLOWER JELLY

Serves 4

For this delectable and stunningly beautiful flower jelly use all the most highly scented petals you can get like violets, roses, pinks, honeysuckle and so on.

To get a really good flavoured jelly it is best to use real fruit. Stand 450g/1lb raspberries or strawberries in a double boiler and heat gently, pouring off the juice as it forms. When you have extracted all the juice you can, sweeten if necessary and make up to 600ml/1 pint by adding water.

Dissolve 15g/½oz (1 tablespoon) powdered gelatine (2 envelopes) in 6 tablespoons of very hot water. Pour the juice into the gelatine, bit by bit.

Choose a pretty glass bowl and pour a little of the jelly into it, then add some flower petals, tucking them well down the side of the bowl so that they show through the glass. Add some more jelly as it begins to set, and more flowers until the bowl is full.

Serve slightly chilled with some wicked clotted cream, and butter cookies.

FLOWER FRITTERS

Makes about 12 fritters

Flowers go extremely well with a light batter, especially those with a strong fragrance, such as nasturtiums, elderflowers, tiger lilies and honeysuckle. Squash and courgette (zucchini) flowers also make delicious fritters. Why not make a pretty display of different flower fritters arranged on a plate with some fresh flowers tucked in between them? They taste superb.

Batter

8oz/225g (2 cups) flour
8fl oz/225ml (1 cup) milk
8fl oz/225ml (1 cup) water
2 eggs, beaten
1 tablespoon oil
1 tablespoon sugar
1/4 teaspoon salt

assortment of flowers
oil, for deep frying
sugar and lemon juice, to serve

First make the batter. Sift the flour into a large bowl. Mix together the milk and water and gradually pour it into the flour, beating with a wooden spoon until smooth. Beat in the beaten eggs, oil, sugar and salt and leave the batter in a cool place for about 2 hours before using.

To make the fritters, dip the flowers in the batter and deep fry quickly in hot oil. Drain on kitchen paper and serve very hot sprinkled with sugar and lemon juice.

CRÈME PÂTISSIÈRE WITH CRYSTALLIZED VIOLETS OR PRIMROSES

Serves 6

This is a dessert for a special occasion. Serve it in tall frosted glasses (chill the glasses in the refrigerator just before serving) and place the crystallized flowers carefully on top. Serve with almond biscuits or *langues de chat*, if you like.

5 egg yolks
6oz/175g (⅔ cup) sugar
3oz/75g (¾ cup) flour
15fl oz/425ml (1⅞ cups) milk
1 tablespoon unsalted (sweet) butter
1½ teaspoons real vanilla essence
crystallized violets or primroses, to decorate

In a large bowl, beat together the egg yolks and sugar until pale yellow and creamy. Sift in the flour and gradually beat it into the mixture.

Bring the milk to the boil and gradually add it to the egg mixture, beating continuously.

Pour the custard mixture into a clean, heavy pan and place over moderate heat. Bring to the boil, whisking continuously with a balloon whisk.

Boil gently for 2 minutes, whisking all the time, until the custard is thick enough to coat the back of a spoon.

Take the pan off the heat and beat in the butter, then stir in the vanilla essence. Pour the crème pâtissière into tall glasses and leave to cool. Cover the glasses with cling film to prevent a skin from forming. Chill in the fridge and decorate with crystallized flowers just before serving.

SWEET BERRY PANCAKES FILLED WITH SUMMER FLOWERS

Serves 8

These filled pancakes make a superb dessert on a summer's day. I always add a side dish of thick yogurt to serve with them; I can guarantee that everyone will want more and more!

You can use any summer berries for the filling (red and black currants are particularly good). Make the batter several hours in advance.

Batter

8oz/225g (2 cups) plain flour
8fl oz/225ml (1 cup) milk
7fl oz/200ml (⅞ cup) water
2 eggs
1 tablespoon sunflower oil
1 tablespoon caster sugar
¼ teaspoon salt

fresh berries, for filling
caster sugar and fresh summer flowers, to serve

Sift the flour into a large bowl and make a well in the centre. Mix together the milk and water and very gradually pour the mixture into the flour, beating all the time with a wooden spoon until the mixture is smooth.

In another bowl, whisk the eggs and add them to the flour, together with the oil, sugar and salt. Whisk thoroughly, then leave to stand for 3–4 hours.

Grease a pancake pan with a little oil, pour in about 2 tablespoons of batter and cook until golden underneath. Toss or turn the pancake and cook until the second side is golden. Repeat the process until all the batter is used up, keeping the cooked pancakes warm over a pan of simmering water.

Fill each pancake with berries, sprinkle with caster sugar and a few summer flowers. Serve at once.

ICE CREAMS AND SORBETS

Flowers can flavour both real cream ices and sorbets with great delicacy and subtlety. Cream ices are made by steeping the petals in the cream for some time before the final whipping process. Flower sorbets are usually made with sieved fruit, with perhaps a little added citrus fruit juice, sweetened with a sugar syrup in which the flowers have been steeped. Both ice creams and sorbets give excellent results when made with flowers and they can look really beautiful decorated with either fresh or crystallized flower petals.

Fruit juice sorbets are an easy way to incorporate flowers. You can use ¾pt/425ml (2 cups) of juice with enough flower sugar syrup to dilute. Gin and liqueurs are perfect additions for that extra special taste. Fresh flowers can be used to flavour and decorate.

Ice creams and sorbets should be served in really beautiful glasses or, for a special occasion, you can make flower ice bowls. The ice creams and sorbets will look stunning in the flower-strewn ice bowls and these will certainly become a talking point at any dinner party (see opposite).

All the recipes given here can be made in an ice cream maker or sorbetière, if you are lucky enough to own one; obviously they will not require beating during the freezing process.

FLOWER ICE BOWLS

A delightful way to serve ice creams and sorbets is in a flower ice bowl. These are beautiful to look at and a novel idea for special occasions like weddings. The frozen ice bowl is decorated with flowers and is quite simple to make.

Take 2 freezer-proof bowls, one of which should be about two-thirds smaller than the other. Put some ice cubes in the larger bowl and put the smaller bowl on top of the ice cubes. Pour iced water into the gap between the two bowls. Now strew in lots of flowers and petals. Use a variety of summer flowers like rose petals, lilac, honeysuckle, primroses, herb flowers and lilies. Put in ice cubes on top of the flowers to keep them from floating to the surface. You can make several layers of ice cubes and flowers which will give an ice bowl with a wonderful decorative effect.

Weight down the smaller bowl and place the assembled bowls in the freezer for at least 6 hours. To unmould, remove the weights from the small bowl and pour in a little lukewarm water. Lift out the smaller bowl, dip the bottom of the larger bowl in lukewarm water and unmould it.

Serve ices or sorbets in the ice flower bowls immediately, placing a napkin underneath each one to absorb any water. They will certainly be the talking point of your party!

WHITE AND YELLOW ROSE PETAL ICE CREAM WITH CRYSTALLIZED ROSE PETALS

I like this ice cream because it has the delicate perfume of roses. Decorate with crystallized white and yellow petals instead of the more usual pink or red.

Set off the ice cream by placing it on a bed of bright green rose leaves. It will create quite a stir among your guests – and it tastes marvellous.

Make an ice cream exactly as for Vanilla ice cream (see page 123), but substitute 6 tablespoons white and yellow rose petals for the vanilla pod. You can add a little rose oil and/or rose water for extra flavour or, if you have a rose liqueur, add a little of that.

SCENTED-LEAVED GERANIUM ICE CREAM

Serves 6

This delectable ice cream should be made in mid-summer when you can choose from the many kinds of scented-leaved geraniums (*pelargoniums*) to make the ice cream. They all have different scents, so choose one which pleases you for an exciting taste. Serve the ice cream scattered with fresh petals.

Don't cheat and try to make it with ordinary geraniums – it will taste horrid!

½pt/275ml single cream (1¼ cups light cream)
6 sweet-scented geranium (pelargonium) *leaves, bruised*
1 tablespoon sweet-scented geranium petals
4 egg yolks
2oz/50g (½ cup) caster sugar
½pt/275ml double cream (1¼ cups heavy cream)
sweet-scented geranium leaves and petals, to decorate

Pour the single (light) cream into a heavy pan, add the bruised geranium leaves and a few petals and slowly bring to the boil. Remove from the heat, cover the pan and leave in a warm place to infuse for about 30 minutes.

Whisk together the egg yolks and sugar, then whisk in the infused cream. Pour the mixture into the pan and cook over low heat, stirring continuously, until the custard is thick enough to coat the back of a wooden spoon. Remove the leaves and petals and leave the custard to cool.

Beat the double (heavy) cream until fairly stiff. Add the cooled custard and mix gently. Pour the mixture into an ice tray and freeze until the edges are just firm. Stir well with a fork, turning the edges into the middle and freeze until the ice cream is all one consistency, but not completely hard. Turn it out into a bowl and whisk well. Return it to the ice tray and freeze until quite firm.

Remove the ice cream from the freezer about 1 hour before serving. Serve attractive scoops in pretty glass dishes and scatter over tiny scented geranium petals. Tuck a fresh leaf into each dish and serve with shortcake biscuits.

MINT FLOWER ICE CREAM

Serves 4–6

This is a perfect dessert for a summer's day. Usc a combination of spearmint, apple mint and eau-de-cologne mint for the best flavour.

4oz/100g (½ cup) caster sugar
5fl oz/150ml (⅜ cup) water
3–4 tablespoons mint leaves
1 teaspoon mint flowers
juice ½ lemon
½pt/275ml double cream (1¼ cups heavy cream)
green food colouring, optional
mint leaves and flowers, to decorate

Dissolve the sugar in the water, then boil for 3–4 minutes to make a light syrup. Put in the mint leaves and flowers and liquidize until smooth.

Cool, then strain. Add the lemon juice and stir in the cream. Mix well together, whisking gently. Add a drop or two of food colouring if necessary.

Pour into an ice tray and freeze until mushy. Beat well, then freeze until hard.

Serve in tall glasses, decorated with sprigs of mint leaves and lots of fresh mint flowers.

AMARETTI ICE CREAM WITH CRYSTALLIZED LAVENDER FLOWERS

This is a delicious variation on the vanilla ice cream recipe given on page 123. I was introduced to this delectable ice cream by a friend who knew my penchant for amaretti biscuits. It is perfectly simple to make and wonderfully crunchy to eat.

Crumble about 6oz/150g amaretti into 1pt/575ml (2½ cups) homemade Vanilla ice cream (see page 123) and mix well together. Crystallize some fresh lavender sprigs (see page 6) and serve the ice cream in blue and white bowls, with the lavender sprigs decorating each one. It tastes superb.

GLÂCE DE JASMIN

Serves 4

3 tablespoons freshly picked jasmine flowers
5 fl oz/150ml (³⁄₈ cup) boiling water
4oz/100g (¹⁄₂ cup) caster sugar
juice ¹⁄₂ lemon
¹⁄₂pt/275ml double cream (1¹⁄₄ cups)
yellow food colouring, optional
jasmine flowers, to decorate

Place half the jasmine flowers in the boiling water and leave for 1 hour.

Dissolve the sugar in the jasmine water, then bring to the boil and boil for 4–5 minutes, until syrupy. Strain the syrup and place in a blender or food processor. Add the remaining flowers and liquidize. Cool, then add the lemon juice. Add the cream and whisk lightly, adding a tiny drop of yellow colouring, if you wish.

Pour into an ice tray and freeze until the edges are just firm. Transfer to a bowl, beat thoroughly, then pour back into the tray and freeze.

Remove the ice cream from the freezer 1 hour before serving. Decorate with lots of jasmine flowers and eat with sugar biscuits.

V·ANILLA ICE CREAM WITH PEACHES MARINATED IN ROSE BRANDY

Serves 6

6 fresh peaches
8fl oz/225ml (1 cup) rose brandy
½pt/275ml single cream (1¼ cups light cream)
1 vanilla pod
4 egg yolks
2oz/50g (½ cup) caster sugar
½pt/275ml double cream (1¼ cups heavy cream), lightly whipped
pink rose petals, to decorate

Plunge the peaches into boiling water for 2 minutes, skin, halve and stone. Place in a dish, pour over enough rose brandy to cover and leave to marinate overnight.

Make the ice cream: pour the single (light) cream into a saucepan, put in the vanilla pod and heat until the cream is just warm. Leave for 20 minutes, then bring to the boil and remove from the heat. Cover the pan and leave for a further 20 minutes. Remove the vanilla pod (wash and dry it for use another time).

Whisk together the egg yolks and sugar, then whisk in the vanilla flavoured cream. Pour the mixture back into the pan and cook over low heat, stirring continuously, until the custard is thick enough to coat the back of a wooden spoon. Leave to cool.

Beat the double (heavy) cream until fairly stiff. Add the cooled custard and mix gently. Pour the mixture into an ice tray and freeze until the edges are just firm. Stir briskly, turning the edges into the middle and freeze until the ice cream is all one consistency but not completely hard. Turn out into a bowl and whisk with an electric beater until quite firm.

Remove the ice cream from the freezer about 1 hour before serving. Lay 2 marinated peach halves in shallow glass dessert dishes and cover with the ice cream. Put a pink rose petal on each mound of ice cream and pour over a little more rose brandy.

REDCURRANT SORBET WITH THYME FLOWERS

Serves 4

This sorbet has a lovely pinky-red colour and the tiny mauve thyme flowers make an attractive contrast.

1lb/450g redcurrants, cooked
3–4 tablespoons orange juice
Sugar syrup (see page 127)
redcurrants, caster sugar and thyme flowers, to serve

Sieve the cooked redcurrants, stir in the orange juice and sweeten to taste with sugar syrup. Pour into an ice tray and freeze until the edges are just firm, then beat thoroughly.

Return the sorbet to the ice tray and freeze until hard.

Remove from the freezer about 1 hour before serving. Serve the sorbet in glass dishes, decorated with redcurrants dipped in caster sugar and lots of thyme flowers.

LEMON BALM AND ELDERFLOWER SORBET

Serves 4

Juice and thinly pared rinds 3 lemons
6oz/175g (¾ cup) caster sugar
1pt/575ml (2½ cups) water
2 sprigs lemon balm
3–4 sprays elderflowers
1 egg white
elderflowers, lemon balm and twists of lemon peel, to garnish

In a heavy pan, combine the lemon rinds, sugar, water, lemon balm and elderflowers. Set over low heat and stir until all the sugar has dissolved. Bring to the boil and boil for 5 minutes. Add the lemon juice, then strain the liquid, pour into an ice tray and freeze until slushy.

Place in a blender or food processor and blend until smooth. Beat the egg white until stiff, then fold it into the sorbet mixture and mix thoroughly. Return the sorbet to the ice tray and freeze until the edges are firm. Beat once more and freeze until hard.

Remove the sorbet from the freezer about 1 hour before you want to eat it. Decorate with elderflowers, twists of lemon peel and a sprig of lemon balm.

ROSE PETAL SORBET WITH CRYSTALLIZED ROSE PETALS

Serves 6

Joyce Molyneux of the Carved Angel restaurant in Dartmouth, Devon makes this mouth-watering sorbet, prettily decorated with crystallized pink rose petals.

Sorbet

8oz/225g (1 cup) sugar
½pt/275ml (1¼ cups) water
petals of 3 large scented roses
½pt/275ml (1¼ cups) white wine
juice 2 lemons

Crystallized petals

1 teaspoon gum arabic
2 tablespoons vodka
caster sugar

Make a sugar syrup by dissolving the sugar in the water. Bring to the boil and boil for 4–5 minutes.

Place the rose petals and white wine in a blender or food processor together with the lemon juice and the sugar syrup and liquidize. Pour into an ice tray and freeze until mushy. Beat well, then freeze until hard.

To crystallize the rose petals, combine the gum arabic and vodka and dip each petal into the mixture. Sprinkle with caster sugar and leave on a rack to dry overnight.

Serve the sorbet decorated with the crystallized rose petals.

EXOTIC LAVENDER SORBET

Serves 8

A recipe from John McGeever of Congham Hall in Norfolk.

2 ripe Ogen melons
juice 2 lemons
4oz/100g (½ cup) caster sugar
½ bottle dry sparkling wine or champagne
1 tablespoon lavender flowers
2 egg whites
blue food colouring
fresh lavender flowers, to decorate

Scoop out the melon flesh and discard the seeds. Place the flesh in a blender or food processor with the lemon juice and sugar and liquidize.

Slightly warm the wine, put in the lavender flowers and infuse for about 12 minutes. Strain the liquid, pressing it through muslin to extract as much liquid as possible. Add the liquid to the puréed melons and stir in 1–2 drops of blue food colouring. Beat the egg whites until stiff, then fold into the sorbet mixture.

Pour into an ice tray and freeze until mushy, then beat the mixture until smooth and freeze until hard.

Remove from the freezer 1 hour before serving and decorate with fresh lavender flowers.

FRESH JUNE STRAWBERRY SORBET WITH TINY WHITE ROSE PETALS

Make this sorbet following the recipe for Redcurrant sorbet (see page 124), but using uncooked, sieved strawberries. Add just enough sugar to sweeten a little and a very small quantity of lemon juice for 'bite'.

Serve this perfect summer sorbet in pretty scoops and decorate with the tiniest white rose petals you can find.

CRANBERRY SORBET WITH WHITE STOCKS

Serves 4–6

This sorbet is delicious served in scooped-out orange halves, with the orange segments arranged alternately with small scoops of sorbet. Serve it with madeleines.

zest and juice 1 orange
zest and juice 1 lemon
8oz/225g cranberries
1pt/575ml (2½ cups) water
6oz/150g (¾ cup) caster sugar
1 egg white
1 tablespoon white stock petals

In a heavy pan, combine the orange and lemon zest, cranberries and water. Simmer for 10–12 minutes, until the cranberries are tender. Rub through a fine wire sieve, then stir the sugar into the juice until dissolved, and add the stocks. Pour into an ice tray and freeze until mushy.

Whisk the egg white until stiff, beat the sorbet thoroughly, then fold in the beaten egg white and freeze the sorbet until hard.

Serve decorated with lots of highly scented white stock petals and eat with madeleines.

SUGAR SYRUP

Makes about 1pt/575ml (2½ cups)

½pt/275ml (1¼ cups) water
1lb/450g (2 cups) granulated sugar

Bring the water to the boil, then put in the sugar and stir well until the sugar has dissolved completely. Bring the syrup back to the boil, lower the heat and simmer for 1–2 minutes.

CAKES AND BISCUITS

Cakes stuffed with flowers, like the Christmas one (page 70), or decorated with frothy cream and tiny scented buds or petals like the Strawberry sponge (page 131), are real treats. Crystallized flowers, of course, are a perfect ingredient for decorating any cake, from the grandest, most elegant wedding cake to the richest chocolate gâteau. Use a combination of crystallized and fresh flowers for the best effect. You can use your creative skills to the utmost here and you will get enormous fun from doing so.

Remember to dry your favourite scented flowers during the summer months when they are at their best, then you will have them in the autumn and winter and your cakes will bring back memories of the lovely colours and flavours of summer.

Biscuits, too, can be prettily decorated with either fresh or crystallized petals or buds. Let the children help you to make them; they will be thrilled to offer their friends a plate of biscuits decorated with rose petals, lavender flowers and hibiscus.

MERINGUE CAKE WITH FRESH EXOTIC FRUITS AND FLOWERS

Serves 6–8

This 'cake' has a lovely, crunchy meringue base and is topped by folds of whipped cream and flavoured with fresh fruits and flowers. You can let your imagination run wild here and make the creamy top into a dazzling picture combining exotic, different coloured fruits with whatever wonderful flowers are available at the time you make it. Serve it as a stunning dessert decorated with a garland of fresh flowers around the plate.

3 large egg whites
6oz/175g (³⁄₄ cup) caster sugar
oil, for greasing
8 fl oz/225ml double cream (1 cup heavy cream)
fresh fruits (eg: kiwi, passion fruit, pineapple, banana, peach, pear, grapes, oranges)
fresh flowers (eg: borage, mint, honeysuckle, English cowslips, primroses, pansies, rose petals)

Heat the oven to 300F/150C/gas 2.

In a large clean bowl, whisk the egg whites until they form stiff peaks. Whisk in the sugar, about a tablespoon at a time, until the mixture is thoroughly amalgamated and fairly stiff.

Oil a large baking sheet and line it with oiled greaseproof paper or non-stick baking parchment. Spoon the meringue mixture onto the paper in a large, even circle. Bake in the oven for 5–10 minutes, then reduce the temperature to 275F/140C/gas 1 and cook for a further 50 minutes. Turn off the oven and leave the meringue there for another few hours to dry out completely.

When the meringue is cool, whip the cream until thick and pile it on top of the meringue. Add the fruits and flowers in an attractive pattern and serve this exotic picture 'cake' to your delighted guests!

TEATIME SPONGE WITH DAISIES

Makes 1 × 8in/20cm cake

This is a delightfully pretty cake for a special teatime. Decorate it with fresh daisies* or with crystallized flowers.

Any sponge recipe is suitable for this cake – use your own favourite recipe or the one below and ice the cake with smooth white icing. Sandwich the sponge together with jam, cream or buttercream.

4oz/100g (½ cup) butter or *sunflower margarine*
4oz/100g (1 cup) caster sugar
2 eggs
4oz/100g self-raising (1 cup all purpose) flour
filling, white icing and fresh or crystallized flowers to serve

Heat the oven to 375F/190C/gas 5. Grease an 8in/20cm cake tin.

Cream together the butter and sugar until very light and fluffy. In a separate bowl, beat the eggs, then gradually beat them into the butter mixture, beating all the time. Sift in the flour and fold it into the mixture with a metal spoon.

Pour into the prepared cake tin and bake for 20 minutes. When cooked, turn out onto a wire rack and leave to cool. Slice in half and fill with buttercream. Ice with plain white icing and decorate with fresh or crystallized flowers just before serving.

*Only eat if *Bellis perennis* (i.e. the common English daisy).

STRAWBERRY SPONGE WITH ROSE PETALS

Serves 6–8

4oz/100g (½ cup) butter or *sunflower margarine*
4oz/100g (½ cup) caster sugar
2 large eggs
4oz/100g self-raising flour (1 cup all-purpose flour), sifted
1lb/450g fresh strawberries
2 tablespoons highly scented rose petals
1pt/575ml double cream (2½ cups heavy cream)
caster or *icing (confectioner's) sugar, to serve*

Heat the oven to 350F/180C/gas 4.

Grease and lightly flour two 8in/20cm shallow cake tins.

Cream the butter and sugar together until the mixture is very light, fluffy and pale. Whisk the eggs in a separate bowl and gradually add them to the butter mixture, beating all the time. Fold in the sifted flour with a metal spoon.

Divide the cake mixture between the two tins and bake in the oven for 20–25 minutes. To test if the sponges are cooked, gently slide a knife into the centre. If it comes out clean, the cakes are ready.

Remove the cakes from the tins and cool on a wire rack.

Hull the strawberries and tear the rose petals into pieces. Whip the cream until it is very thick.

When the cakes have cooled, stir 1 tablespoon of torn rose petals into half the whipped cream and sandwich the sponges together with this mixture. Cover the top of the cake with the rest of the cream, decorate with rose petals and then add a thick layer of strawberries. Cover with a dusting of caster or icing (confectioner's) sugar and serve to your guests on a glass plate surrounded by more rose petals.

FLOWER COOKIES

Makes 16–20 cookies

These teatime biscuits (cookies) are cut into flower shapes and topped with an assortment of different crystallized whole flowers or petals. Serve them for a special party or summer teatime, arranged on your best china plate. Make the biscuits from your own favourite mixture or the one below.

4oz/100g (¹/₂ cup) butter, plus a little for greasing
4oz/100g (¹/₂ cup) caster sugar
1 egg, beaten
8oz/225g (2 cups) plain flour
flour, for dusting
crystallized flowers, to decorate (see page 6)

Cream the butter and sugar until light and fluffy (you can do this in a blender). Add the egg and sift in the flour. Mix with a wooden spoon until you have a firm dough. Wrap in cling film or polythene and chill in the fridge for about 1 hour.

Heat the oven to 375F/190C/gas 5.

On a lightly floured surface, roll out the dough and cut out flower shapes with pastry cutters or a sharp knife. Put a crystallized flower on each cookie and place on a greased baking sheet. Cook in the oven for 10–15 minutes, until they are just turning brown at the edges. Cool on a wire rack.

HIBISCUS AND ORANGE FINGER BISCUITS (COOKIES) WITH CINNAMON

Makes about 24

10oz/275g (2½ cups) plain flour
1 teaspoon baking powder (baking soda)
5oz/150g (⅝ cup) butter or sunflower margarine, plus a little for greasing
5oz/150g (⅝ cup) caster sugar
grated zest 1 orange
2 tablespoons purple hibiscus petals, torn
1 large egg, beaten
¼ teaspoon ground cinnamon
caster or icing (confectioner's) sugar and fresh hibiscus petals, to serve

Heat the oven to 350F/180C/gas 4. Lightly grease a baking sheet.

Sift the flour and baking powder (baking soda) into a large, warmed bowl. Set aside.

In another bowl, cream together the butter and sugar until very pale and creamy. Add the grated orange zest, hibiscus petals and the beaten egg and mix thoroughly. Add the cinnamon, then fold in the flour mixture, mixing well to form a firm dough. Wrap in cling film and chill in the fridge for 15 minutes.

On a lightly floured surface, roll out the dough and cut into fingers. Place these on the greased baking sheet and bake for 10–15 minutes, until lightly coloured.

Transfer the biscuits to a wire rack and leave to cool a little. Serve slightly warm, dusted with caster or icing (confectioner's) sugar and decorated with fresh hibiscus flowers.

FLOWER DRINKS – HOT AND COLD

Flowers make perfect companions for both hot and cold drinks. The warm scents of flowers like violets and roses can enhance hot and spicy drinks, while cool summer concoctions look and taste wonderful with the addition of borage, lemon verbena, jasmine, sweet woodruff and many others. Here are a few recipes to start you off, but I am sure that once your imagination gets going you will create many more.

Wassail

Inevitably this grand drink is consumed mainly at Christmas time round a crackling fire accompanied by laughter and singing. You will have to use dried rose petals with the apples to flavour the Wassail but if you choose properly dried and highly scented petals the effect will be just as good as using fresh rose petals.

Into a large saucepan put 1 cup water, 4 cups sugar, 2 teaspoons ground ginger, 1 tablespoon freshly grated nutmeg, ¼ teaspoon ground mace, 6 whole cloves, 6 allspice berries, 1 whole stick cinnamon and a handful of dried rose petals. Bring to the boil and simmer for 5 minutes.

Beat 12 egg whites until they form soft peaks. Whisk the egg yolks separately. Fold the egg whites into the yolks and pour into the hot spicy mixture in the pan, stirring all the time.

In a separate pan, bring to the boil 4 bottles cheap sweet sherry and 2 cups cooking brandy. Slowly mix the hot sherry and brandy with the spicy mixture in the large pan. Just before serving add some hot baked apples.

Make sure your guests are seated by the fire then serve the Wassail in a large, warmed tureen and ladle it out into thick heatproof bowls or glasses, giving each guest a spoon with which to eat the delicious frothy apples which will have sunk to the bottom.

Pimms with Borage Leaves and Flowers

In a glass jug, measure for each person 1 measure Pimms, 1 glass fizzy lemonade, a sprig of borage and some borage flowers. Make as much as you like, using the same proportions and adding slices of cucumber and orange and lots and lots of ice cubes.

This is a traditional English drink for summer days and it really is my favourite. What could be nicer and more refreshing than sipping a Pimms in the shade of leafy trees in an English garden in high summer?

Home-made Lemonade with Lemon Balm and Mint Flowers

Thinly pare 5 good-sized lemons and put the peel into a bowl. Pour over

1pt/575ml (2½ cups) boiling water. Squeeze the lemons and strain the juice into the bowl. Add 1½lb/700g (3 cups) white sugar and stir until it dissolves. Leave for about 8 hours, then strain.

Stir in 1 tablespoon citric acid, then bottle the lemonade in screw top jars and keep in the refrigerator. It will keep well for about 3 weeks.

Serve the lemonade diluted to your taste with plenty of ice cubes, a sprig of lemon balm and a scattering of mauve mint flowers. It is very cooling on a hot, sultry day.

Summer Ale Cup with Sweet Woodruff
This is sometimes called a 'cool tankard' and very refreshing it is.

Pour 1 bottle chilled Moselle or medium sweet white wine or cider onto a large bunch of sweet woodruff and stand it on ice for at least 30 minutes. Dissolve 2oz/50g (¼ cup) sugar in 5fl oz/150ml (⅝ cup) water and mix with the wine or cider. Remove the woodruff and add some slices of orange or lemon.

Serve in tankards with fresh sprigs of flowering woodruff.

Elderflower Champagne
Pick 6–8 large heads of flowering elderflower when they are quite dry and free of insects. Boil 1 gallon/4.5L (20 cups) water and when boiling remove from the heat and dissolve 1¼lb/600g (2½ cups) sugar in it. When cool put in the elderflowers, 2 sliced lemons and 2 tablespoons white wine vinegar. Leave for 24–48 hours. Strain into strong glass bottles and cork tightly. It may be wise to wire down the corks, since this is fizzy stuff! It is ready to drink in about 6 days.

This is a delightful and most refreshing drink in summer, and often quite heady! Serve it well chilled.

Chilled Rosé Punch with Rose Petals
Chill a bottle of rosé wine in a glass bowl with a handful of scented rose petals – white and pink mixed make a good show. Add 4 tablespoons vodka, several raspberries and lots of ice cubes. Chill for 1 hour, then add 1 bottle of carbonated mineral water before serving.

This is an excellent drink for summer cocktail parties, especially as it is not strong enough to go to one's head too quickly!

TISANES

Flower teas, or *tisanes* as they are known, are not only pleasant to drink but are often beneficial medicinally as well. With the current fashion of trying to avoid too much caffeine, contained in normal teas, *tisanes* are becoming much easier to obtain in the shops, but it is very simple to make your own herbal teas from either fresh or dried flowers.

The old gardens were originally 'physic' gardens where herbs and flowers were often grown for their medicinal properties as well as for their oils, perfumes and culinary virtues. Before the advent of medicines, people drank herbal teas to help cure all kinds of ailments. Today we are reviving that habit and also taking great pleasure in the sheer delight of tasting all kinds of *tisanes*.

Here I have given examples of just a few of the many flower teas available. Since this is a book about flowers, I have mentioned only teas made from flowers, although many herb leaves may be used as well.

To make a *tisane* you should use 1 teaspoon of fresh or dried flowers to 1 cup of boiling water. Pour the water over the flowers and leave to infuse for about 4 minutes, then strain and drink. You can add a slice of lemon and a little honey if you like, but never drink *tisanes* with milk — the two just do not go together.

Rose Petal

Rose petals have such a lovely taste that we all probably just enjoy a warm rose *tisane* without thinking too much about the medicinal properties. As you might expect, rose petals are said to 'cheer the heart' — and what could be nicer?

Lavender

Well known as a 'cure' for headaches. It is also beneficial to those suffering from nervous tension and strain. It makes a lovely tea with a heady scent.

Elderflower

This is excellent taken internally as well as externally for the skin. It is said that if splashed over freckles, they will disappear!

Hyssop

Hyssop is often used by those suffering from colds or sore throats. It is also a good *tisane* to drink; serve it chilled on a hot day since it has a nicely cooling effect.

Lime Blossom

This is the standard *tisane* of France. Called *tilleul* it is often given to patients in hospital to help induce sleep in preference to sleeping pills. The creamy blossoms have a soothing effect and can be helpful in reducing fevers.

Dandelion

A *tisane* of the flower head will help reduce headaches and relieve gall bladder pain. It is slightly diuretic and can be helpful to those suffering from water retention.

Chamomile

One of the most popular flower teas. This is also a gentle, sedative *tisane* which will help to induce sleep if taken 1 hour before bedtime. It is also soothing for heartburn and good as a tonic.

The flowers are excellent as a hair tonic too and help to keep fair hair light. A hair rinse is made by steeping 2 tablespoons of chamomile flowers in 1pt/575ml (2½ cups) boiling water for 1–2 hours. You then strain the liquid and pour repeatedly over freshly washed hair.

Passiflora

The exotic passion flower which, again, is mildly sedative, is often given to those suffering from nerves.

Jasmine

Simply a most delicious perfumed tea. Good cold or hot, served with a slice of orange instead of lemon.

Peppermint

Use both flowers and leaves. It is well known as being the best digestive there is and can settle a child's upset stomach quickly. Serve chilled on a summer's day when it will be most refreshing and often acts as a 'pick-me-up' for those who are exhausted.

Hibiscus and Rosemary

Both these *tisanes* may be taken on their own and are delicious. Together they are exotic and refreshing, good for those suffering with their nerves and also used as an aphrodisiac!

GLOSSARY OF EDIBLE FLOWERS

All flowers marked with a * should be eaten only in the amounts specified in the recipes

Common name	Latin name	Family	Flowering time
Anchusa	*Anchusa azurea* *Anchusa officinalis*	*Boraginaceae*	Summer
Basil, Sweet	*Ocimum basilicum*	*Labiatae*	Summer
Bergamot, Red	*Monarda didyma*	*Labiatae*	Summer
Borage	*Borago officinalis*	*Boraginaceae*	Summer
Carnation and Clove Pink	*Dianthus caryophyllus*	*Caryophyllaceae*	Spring, Summer and Autumn
Chamomile	*Anthemis nobilis*	*Compositae*	Summer
Chervil	*Anthriscus cerefolium*	*Umbelliferae*	Summer
Chickweed	*Stellaria media*	*Caryophyllaceae*	Spring, Summer and Autumn
Chicory	*Cichorium intybus*	*Compositae*	Spring, Summer and Autumn
Chive	*Allium schoenoprasum*	*Liliaceae*	Summer
Chrysanthemum	*Chrysanthemum* species	*Compositae*	Autumn
Clover, Red	*Trifolium pratense*	*Leguminosae*	Summer
Cornflower (Bachelor's button)	*Centaurea cyanus*	*Compositae*	Summer and Autumn
Courgette	*Cucurbita pepo*	*Cucurbitaceae*	Summer
Cowslip (do *not* eat American equivalent)	*Primula veris*	*Primulaceae*	Spring
Dandelion	*Taraxacum officinale*	*Compositae*	Spring, Summer and Autumn
Daisy (do *not* eat American equivalent)	*Bellis perennis*	*Compositae*	Spring, Summer and Autumn
Dill	*Anethum graveolens*	*Umbelliferae*	Summer
Fennel	*Foeniculum vulgare*	*Umbelliferae*	Summer
Hawthorn	*Crataegus monogyna*	*Rosaceae*	Spring
*Heartsease	*Viola tricolor*	*Violaceae*	Spring and Summer
Hibiscus	*Hibiscus rosa-sinensis*	*Malvaceae*	Summer
Hollyhock	*Althaea rosea*	*Malvaceae*	Summer
Honeysuckle	*Lonicera* species	*Caprifoliaceae*	Spring
Hop	*Humulus lupulus*	*Cannabaceae*	Summer
*Grape Hyacinth	*Muscari neglectum*	*Liliaceae*	Spring
Hyssop	*Hyssopus officinalis*	*Labiatae*	Summer
Jasmine	*Jasminum* species	*Oleaceae*	Summer and Autumn

(not to be confused with Carolina jessamine – *Gelsemium sempervirens* – which is poisonous)

Common name	Latin name	Family	Flowering time
Lavender	*Lavandula* species	*Labiatae*	Summer
Lily, Day	*Hemerocallis* species	*Liliaceae*	Summer
Lily, Tiger	*Lilium tigrinum*	*Liliaceae*	Summer
Lime Blossom	*Tilia* x *europaea*	*Tiliaceae*	Summer
Lovage	*Levisticum officinale*	*Umbelliferae*	Summer
Magnolia	*Magnolia grandiflora* and *Magnolia denudata*	*Magnoliaceae*	Spring, Summer and Autumn
Mallow	*Malva* species	*Malvaceae*	Summer
Marsh Mallow	*Althaea officinalis*	*Malvaceae*	Summer
Marjoram	*Origanum vulgare*	*Labiatae*	Summer
Marigold, Pot	*Calendula officinalis*	*Compositae*	Summer
Meadowsweet	*Filipendula ulmaria*	*Rosaceae*	Spring
Mint	*Mentha* species	*Labiatae*	Summer
Mustard, Field	*Sinapis arvensis*	*Cruciferae*	Summer
Nasturtium	*Tropaeolum majus*	*Tropaeolaceae*	Summer and Autumn
*Pansy	*Viola* x *wittrockiana*	*Violaceae*	Spring, Summer and Autumn
Passion Flower	*Passiflora* species	*Passifloraceae*	Summer
Pelargonium (*only* those with scented leaves)	*Pelargonium* species	*Geraniaceae*	Summer
Primrose	*Primula vulgaris*	*Primulaceae*	Spring
Rose	*Rosa* species	*Rosaceae*	Summer
Rosemary	*Rosmarinus officinalis*	*Labiatae*	Summer
Sage	*Salvia officinalis*	*Labiatae*	Summer
Saffron	*Crocus sativus*	*Iridaceae*	Autumn
Sorrel, French	*Rumex scutatus*	*Polygonaceae*	Spring and Summer
Sorrel, Common	*Rumex acetosa*	*Polygonaceae*	Spring and Summer
Squash	*Cucurbita pepo*	*Cucurbitaceae*	Summer
Stocks	*Matthiola* species	*Cruciferae*	Summer
Sweet Cicely	*Myrrhis odorata*	*Umbelliferae*	Summer
Sweet Woodruff	*Galium odoratum*	*Rubiaceae*	Summer
*Tansy	*Chrysanthemum vulgare*	*Compositae*	Summer
Thyme	*Thymus* species	*Labiatae*	Summer
Violet, Sweet	*Viola odorata*	*Violaceae*	Spring

USEFUL BOOKS

Apicius, *The Roman Cookery Book – The Art of Cooking*, Trans.Barbara Flower and Elisabeth Rosenbaum, Harrap, London 1958

Clifton, Claire, *Edible Flowers*, Bodley Head, London 1983

Craig, Elizabeth, *Court Favourites*, Andre Deutsch, London 1953

Culpeper's Complete Herbal, Foulsham, London 1952

Evelyn, John, *Acetaria – A Discourse of Sallets* (1699), Prospect Books Facsimile, London 1979

Garland, Sarah, *The Herb & Spice Book*, Frances Lincoln/Weidenfeld and Nicolson, London 1979

Grieve, Mrs M., *A Modern Herbal*, Jonathan Cape, London 1931

Grigson, Geoffrey, *The Englishman's Flora*, Hart-Davis, MacGibbon, London 1975

Grigson, Jane, *Jane Grigson's Fruit Book*, Michael Joseph, London 1982

James, B., *Wild Fruits, Berries, Nuts and Flowers – 101 Good Recipes for Using Them*, Medici Society, London 1942

Larkom, Joy, *The Salad Garden*, Frances Lincoln Ltd/Windward, London 1984

Leyel, Mrs C.F., *The Gentle Art of Cooking*, Chatto & Windus, London 1925

MacNicol, Mary, *Flower Cookery*, The Macmillan Company and Collier Books, New York, 1972

Richardson, Rosamond, *Hedgerow Cookery*, Penguin Books Ltd, Harmondsworth 1980

Rohde, Eleanor Sinclair, *A Garden of Herbs* (1936), Dover, New York 1969, and *Rose Recipes* (1939), Dover, New York, 1973

Toklas, Alice B., *Aromas and Flavours of Past and Present*, Harper, New York, 1958

White, Florence, *Flowers as Food*, Jonathan Cape, London 1934

WHERE TO BUY FLOWERS AND SEEDS BY MAIL ORDER

John Stevens
Suffolk Herbs
Sawyer's Farm
Little Cornard
Sudbury
Suffolk

Rosemary Titterington
Iden Croft Herb Farm
Frittenden Road
Staplehurst
Kent TN12 0DH

John Chambers
15 Westleigh Road
Barton Seagrave
Kettering
Northants NN15 5AJ

Culpeper Ltd
Hadstock Road
Linton
Cambridge CB1 6NJ

Down to Earth Seeds
Streetfield Farm
Cade Street
Heathfield
East Sussex TN21 9BS

Hollington Nurseries
Woolton Hill
Newbury
Berks

All these suppliers have different stocks so it is best to send for their catalogues. Most of them stock a comprehensive range of herb and flower seeds, some of which are very unusual.

WHERE TO BUY FLOWERS AND SEEDS BY MAIL ORDER (USA)

A complete resource for buying herbs by mail order, *The Herb Buyer's Guide*, is available from the Herb Society of America. For more information write:

Herb Society of America
2 Independence Court
Concord, MA 01742
(617) 371 1486

A complete, nationwide resource for buying seeds and flowers by mail order, *Nursery Sources: Native Plants and Wildflowers*, is available from the New England Wildflower Society. For more information write:

New England Wildflower Society
Garden in the Woods
Hemenway Road
Framingham, MA 01701
(617) 237 4924

INDEX